THANKS FOR
THE BAR.

MW01068772

YOU ENJOYED YOURSELVES.
AND I HOPE YOU ENJOY
THIS BOOK ABOUT MY
GREAT, GREAT GRANDFATHER
AN EARLY PIONEER SETTLER
OF JACKSON'S HOLE.

THANKS AGAIN

Jim Thomas

E. N. WILSON,
"Uncle Nick."

AMONG THE SHOSHONES

by
Elijah Nicholas Wilson

Uncle Nick

A person usually has to give a reason for doing anything. I don't know why but in this case I have two good reasons for having this book reissued. First, it is written first hand by Uncle Nick about a small part of his life, just as he lived it and told in his own words. If he had been a writer he could have written twenty books just on his life.

He had quite a sense of humor. Once he told a story of the near massacre at Wilson during the Indian trouble of 1895 where all the neighbors were forted up, keeping a guard posted around the clock. Just as daylight was breaking the sentinel heard an Indian coming through the willows, waited until the Indian poked his head out of the willows, then fired and ran. He was met by several men from the fort who went back to investigate. Sure enough, his shot had hit right between the eyes! The sentinel took one look and started running for the fort and a few minutes later the rest of the men heard a horse running. They stopped laughing long enough for one of them to say, "That's the last we'll see of Joe for a while." Joe was a good shot for he had hit one of the Wilson women's milk cow's calf dead center!

The Wilson's Uncle Nick, his brother Sylvester, their wives and families had settled in Jackson Hole in 1889 and had been responsible for my grandfather, Charles J. Allen and his nephew Jim May coming to Jackson Hole in 1895, a few days after the calf incident. A great joke to Uncle Nick—but one that was never brought up before the Wilson women as they were still on the warpath.

My second reason: The Wilsons were still there to help out when the Allens, Mays and McBrides arrived to stay in 1896, arriving about the middle of the summer as they had stopped to visit the Driggs, their cousins, in Teton Basin (Pierre's Hole). Without the Wilson's and their help, the first winter would have been really tough.

2005 printing

Published by: **M & M Books**
2150 Sacramento Street
Redding, CA 96001

Printed in the United States by Naturegraph Publishers, Happy Camp, California.

Table of Contents

PREFACE

Perhaps you have read, or heard old frontiers-men tell about the many terrible outrages and bloody massacres that have been committed by the red men upon the early settlers in the valleys of the Rocky Mountains. Many a large emigrant train has been overpowered and every one of the people killed and scalped, and their little children's brains dashed out against a hub of a wagon wheel. Houses have been burned and the inmates murdered; barns and hay-stacks destroyed by fire; and cattle and horses driven off.

Now, my dear friends, I know this to be too true, for I am one of the early settlers of the Rocky Mountains, and I have passed through some of the most heartrending experiences that have ever been described.

I have had many narrow escapes from being killed. I have had my friends shot down by my side, and I have been very badly wounded twice.

I was one of the first pony express riders and stage drivers of the early days, and I have seen some terrible things committed by the low-down Gosiute Indians of Utah and Nevada.

Many a poor boy has been shot from his horse when carrying the express. The stations have been burned and the hostlers killed and scalped. This kind of thing happened very often during a period of about two years.

The Humboldt Indians were considered the most cruel and bloodthirsty Indians of those days. Pocatello was the name of their chief, and in after years I got very well acquainted with him. His small band of about five hundred warriors would attack small trains of emigrants, capture the people, tie them down, and burn their eyes out with red hot irons, cut their ears off, and thus torture them until they died. I have not the language to describe these terrible and bloody crimes, but what I do say shall be the truth, and any of the old timers will bear me out in what I say.

Among the Shoshones

CHAPTER I.

PIONEER DAYS.

I came to Utah in 1850 with my parents when I was a very small boy. We moved to one of the outside settlements where the people were having serious trouble with the Indians. We had to group our houses close together and build a high wall all around them to protect ourselves from the savages. Some of the men would generally have to stand guard while the rest worked in the fields, and even then we lost many of our cattle, and very often some of the people would be killed. We had to keep close watch over our cows during the day, and corral them at night, and place a strong guard around the pen.

We built a log schoolhouse in the center of the town, or fort, and near it we erected a very high pole on which we could run a white flag as a signal if the Indians attempted to run off our cattle, or attack the town, or the men at work in the fields. In the log schoolhouse were two old men that would take turns in stopping there all the time to give the signals if necessary, by raising the flag in day time, or by beating a big drum at night, for we had in the house a large bass drum so that if the Indians should make a raid on the cowpen or the town in the night, one of the guard would notify the man with the drum and he would turn loose on the old thing and make it rattle to beat time.

When the people heard the drum, all the women and children were supposed to rush for the schoolhouse, and the men would hurry for the cow corral or take their places along the wall. Often in the dead hours of night when we would be quietly sleeping, we would be startled by the sound of this old drum. Then you would hear the kids coming and squalling from every direction. You bet, I was there, too. Many a time I have run for that old schoolhouse expecting to be filled with arrows before I could get there. Yes, sir, many is the time I have run for that schoolhouse while clinging to my mother's apron and squalling like sixty.

Those Gosiute Indians were the lowest and most degraded and treacherous tribe in the Rocky Mountains. They would go almost naked in the summer

time, but when winter came, they would take rabbit skins and twist them into a long string like a
rope, and then fold it back and forth and tie the
folds together, and in that way make it into a kind
of robe. This robe was generally all they had to
wear in the day time and all they had to sleep in
at night. They would eat almost anything they
could get.

The Shoshones and the Bannocks were not so
bad. They were cleaner and had many ponies to
ride, and they were not so ugly as the mean Gosiutes that we had so much trouble with.

We could not go outside the wall without en-
dangering our lives, and when we would lie down
at night we would not know what would happen
before morning. That is the way, my dear friends,
we were fixed. We did not know at what time,
what minute, we would all be massacred.

While we were fighting the Indians, the grasshoppers and crickets came down from the mountains, ate every green thing, and left the country as
bare as though there had never been anything
growing in the first place. Fine gardens, crops,
meadows—everything was destroyed and the country left a barren desert. To make the situation
worse, most of the people hadn't supplies enough

even to last until harvest time, but now, alas! there would be no harvest. My kind readers, imagine yourselves a thousand miles from civilization among tribes of hostile Indians, with the sun darkened by grasshoppers, and the earth covered with crickets, and with nothing on hand to eat.

I cannot collect words to describe the misery and suffering of the poor people through those two years. The third year things commenced to look somewhat better. The Indians became friendly, the grasshoppers and crickets disappeared, and the people who could muster a little seed raised a small crop that year. Those of us who were left after the starvation period would gather together and sing, "Oh, hard times, come again no more." During those troublous two years many of our friends had been killed by the Indians and others had died for want of proper food, and clothing to protect them from the severe weather.

My Little Indian Brother

CHAPTER II.

MY LITTLE INDIAN BROTHER.

A few Indians hung around the settlement begging their living. The people thought it best to put them to work, so my father made a bargain with one old Indian to work for him. His family consisted of his wife and one small son about my age.

At that time my father had a small bunch of sheep, and he wanted to move out on his farm, which was two miles from the settlement, so he could take better care of them. The old Indian thought it would be safe to do so, as most of the Indians in the neighborhood were becoming more friendly, and the wild Indians were so far away that it was thought they would not bother us. So we moved out to the farm and father put the Indian boy and myself to herding the sheep. I had no other boy to play with, so Pantsuk, the little Indian boy, and myself became greatly attached to each other. I soon learned to talk his language and Pantsuk and I had great times together for two years, when the poor little fellow took sick. We did all we could for him, but he kept getting worse until he died. It was hard for me to part with my dear little friend. I loved him as much as if he had been my own brother.

After Pantsuk died, I had to herd the sheep by myself. The summer wore along very lonely for me, until about the first of August, when there came a band of Shoshone Indians and camped near where I herded sheep. Some of them could talk the Gosiute language which, thanks to my little Indian brother, I could speak, too. They seemed to take quite a fancy to me and would be with me every chance they could get. They said they liked to hear me talk Indian, for they never heard a white boy talk as well as I did.

One day an Indian came to the place where I was herding sheep. He had with him a little pinto pony which I thought was the prettiest thing I ever saw. The Indian could talk Gosiute very well. He asked me if I did not want to ride the pony. I said that I would like to ride him, but was afraid to, for I had never been on a horse in my life. He said that the pony was very gentle. He helped me on to his back and led him around awhile. The next day he came again with the pinto pony and had me ride it again. Four or five of the Indians came this time

and they would take turns leading the pony with me
on his back. I soon got so I could ride him without
their leading him for me. They kept this up for
several days.

Finally the Indian came one day as he had been
doing and let me ride quite a while, and when I got
tired and gave him back the horse, he asked me if
I did not want to keep him. I told him that I would
sooner have the pony than anything I ever saw. He
said I could have the horse, and I could ride him all
the time, if I would go away with him. I said I was
afraid to go. He said he would take good care of
me and would give me bows and arrows, and all the
good buckskin clothes I wanted, if I would go. I
asked him what they had to eat. He said they had
all kinds of meat and berries and fish, sage chickens,
ducks, geese, and rabbits. I thought this surely beat
herding sheep and living on greens and lumpy-
dick, so I told him I would think the matter over.
When he came the next day I told him that I had
decided to go with him.

In five days they were going to start up north
to meet the rest of their tribe. This Indian was to
hide for two days after the rest had gone and then
meet me at a bunch of willows about a mile above
my father's house after dark with the little pinto

pony. Now, my dear friends, how many little boys of my age, lacking only a few months of being twelve years old, would run away from home and friends and go off with a tribe of wild Indians? You will see that I went with them and it was for two years that I never saw a white man. This was in the month of August, 1856.

CHAPTER III.

OFF WITH THE INDIANS.

The night came at last when we were to start.
Just after dark I slipped away from the house and
started for the bunch of willows where I was to
meet the Indian. When I got there, I found two
indians waiting for me instead of one. The sight
of two of them almost made me weaken and turn
back, but as soon as I saw with them my little pinto
pony it gave me new courage, so I went up to them.
They had an old Indian saddle on the pony, with
very rough rawhide thongs for stirrup straps. At
a signal from them, I mounted my horse and away
we went.

The Indians wanted to ride pretty fast. It was
all right at first, but after a while, I got very tired.
My legs began to hurt me and I wanted to stop, but
they urged me along until the peep of day, when we
stopped by some very salty springs. I was so stiff
and sore that I could not get off my horse, so one
of them lifted me off and stood me on the ground,
but I could not stand up. The rawhide straps had
rubbed all the skin off my legs so that they were

as raw as fresh meat. The Indians told me if I would take off my pants and jump into the salt springs it would make my legs better, but I found that I could not get them off for they were stuck to my legs. After some very severe pain we succeeded in getting my pants off, but not a bit of skin was left for about a foot up my legs. They said: "Come on, now, and get into this water and you will be well in a little while." Well, I jumped into the spring up to my waist. O, gosh! O, blazes! I jumped out again. O, Lordy! O, Lordy! O, Lordy! Well, my dear friends, I cannot describe the sensations in my wounded parts. I jumped and I kicked. I bucked and tore up the ground and mashed down the grass until it looked as if a bunch of sheep had been bedded there. Well, after a half hour, I wore myself out, and fell to the ground, and oh, how I cried! The Indians put down a buffalo robe and rolled me on it and spread a blanket over me. I lay there and cried myself to sleep.

When I awoke, the Indians were sitting by a small fire. They had killed a duck and were broiling it for my breakfast. When they saw that I was awake, they said, "Come and eat some duck." I started to get up, and oh! how sore I was. I began to cry again. They kept coaxing me to come and have something to eat, until finally I got up and went to them, but I had to walk on the wide track. I ate some duck and dried meat and then I felt better. They had the horses all ready and said: "Come and get on your horse." I said I could not ride, that I would walk. They said that they were going a long ways and that I could not walk, but they would try to fix the sadde so it would not hurt me. They put a buffalo robe over the old saddle and put me in it. It was not so bad as I thought it would be. I had no pants on so the soft hair of the buffalo robe was all right. One of them tied my pants to my saddle. That day I lost them and I didn't have another pair on for over two years. I had a blanket over my legs to keep the sun from burning them.

We traveled all day over a country that was more like the bottom of an old lake than anything else, and camped that night by another spring. The Indians pulled me from my horse, piled me down on a robe, started a fire, then caught some fish and broiled them on the coals. Oh, what a fine supper we had that night; The next morning I felt pretty well used up, but I ate some fish and a large chunk of dried elk meat for my breakfast and felt better. Then we started on again. Near mid-afternoon, we saw about six miles ahead of us the Indians we had been trying to catch up with. They had overtaken another large band of Indïans so it looked as if there were an awful lot of them. By the time we caught up with them, they had just stopped and were unpacking, and some of them had their wickiups up. We rode through the camp until we came to a big wickiup where a large, good looking Indian was standing. They said this man was their chief, that I was to stop with him, and that he would be my brother. They said his name was Washakie.

An old squaw came up to my horse and stood looking at me. These two Indians told her that my legs were badly skinned and were very sore. One of the Indians that had brought me told me that this old woman was the chief's mother and that she would be my mother, too, and would be very good to me, then Washakie helped me off my horse. The old squaw came up to me and put her hand on my head and began to say something very pitiful to me, and I began to cry. She cried, too, and taking me by the arm, led me into the wickiup, and pointed to a nice bed that the chief's wife had made for me. I lay down on the bed and sobbed myself to sleep. When I woke up, this new mother of mine brought me some soup and some fresh deer meat to eat, and oh, how good it tasted to me!

The next morning my new mother thought she would give me a good breakfast. They had brought some flour from the settlements so she thought she would make me some bread, such as I had been used to having at home. She had no soda, nothing but flour and water, so you may judge what kind of bread it was. She would have had to whip a hungry dog to make him eat it. Along with the bread she gave me some good, fried sage-chicken, some dried meat, and some fresh service berries. I think she did not like it very well when she found that I did not eat the bread.

That day my mother and the chief's wife started to make me something to wear, for after I had lost by breeches, I had nothing on but an old, thin shirt and a straw hat that had met with an accident and lost part of its brim. The elbows were out of my shirt and it did not have a very long tail, either. The two women worked for several hours and finally got the thing finished and gave it to me to put on. I did not know what to call it, for I had not seen anything like it before, but it may have been what the girls now call a mother-hubbard. It was all right, anyhow, when I got it on and my belt around me to keep the thing close to me, but I had to pull the back up a little above the belt to keep

it from choking me to death when I stooped over.
My dear old mother rubbed my legs with skunk oil
and they got better fast. All of the indians were
very kind to me.

We stayed at this camp for five days to give
me time to get well. It had got noised around by
this time that my legs were vary bad, and one day
when I was out in front of the wickiup, a lot of
kids wanted to see them. One stooped to raise my
mother-hubbard to look at them, and the rest began to laugh, but they didn't laugh long, for I gave
him a kick that sent him winding. Then his mother
came out after me and I thought she was going to
eat me up. She gave me quite a lecture, but I did
not know what she said, so it made no difference to
me. My old mother, hearing the noise, came and,
taking me by the hand, led me into the wickiup and
gave me some dried service berries. I thought that
was pretty good and if that was the way they were
going to treat me, I would kick another one if I
got a chance.

It was not long until I got another chance, for
the next day the kids gathered around me again
and another one about my size went to raise my
mother-hubbard. I fetched him a kick that sent him
about a rod and he gave out a war whoop that you

could have heard a mile. It brought about half of the tribe to see how many I had killed. That kid's mother turned loose on me, too, with her tongue and everlastingly ribbed me up. The chief happened to see the trouble and I think that is what kept me from being cremated. Anyhow, after that the kids left my mother-hubbard alone. My mother began to teach me the Shoshone language, and I got along pretty well. Being able to talk the Gosiute language helped me for the two languages were a good deal alike.

One night the hunters came in loaded with meat, and the next day we started to move. The horses were brought in and among them was my pinto pony. When I saw him it seemed as if I had met some one from home, and I ran up and hugged him as if he had been my sweetheart.

My dear old mother had fixed me up a pretty good saddle and had cushioned it off in fine style to keep it from hurting me. We traveled about fifteen miles that day and camped on a small stream which they called Kohits. Mother told me to wade out into the water and bathe my legs. I said, "Not by a d——n sight, I have had all the baths I want." She said the water would make my legs tough, and when she saw that I wouldn't go into the stream, she brought some cold water and told me to wash them. Then I wanted to know if it was salty. She said it was not a bit salty. So I bathed my legs, and when I found the water didn't hurt me, I waded out into the stream. My brother Washakie said it was "tibi tsi djant," which means, "very good."

CHAPTER IV.

THE GREAT ENCAMPMENT.

It was the custom in those early days for all the Indians of this tribe to come together every three years, and this was the year for them to meet again. We started for the great camp ground, and after traveling for three days, we came to a large river, which they called Piupa (Snake River), where we joined another large band of Indians belonging to the same tribe.

In order to cross the river, the squaws built boats of bul-rushes tied in bundles and the bundles lashed together until there were enough to hold up six or eight hundred pounds. The Indians swam the horses, and some of the little boys rode their horses across. I wanted to swim my horse, but my mother would not let me. We spent about a week in getting across the river, and during this time I had more fun than I ever had before in my life.

My mother gave me a fish hook and a line that was made out of hair from a horse's tail. With these I caught my first fish, and some of them were

very large ones, too. I had lots of fun with the
other boys and we became very friendly, but my
mother kept pretty close around for fear I would
kick some of their heads off. After that I learned
to talk Shoshone faster by playing with the kids
than I did from my mother.

Nothing of importance happened until we got
to Big Hole Basin. There I saw the first buffalo I
had seen since I crossed the plains. One morning
we saw seven head on the bench about a mile away.
Ten Indians started after them. One having a wide
spear with a long handle would ride up to a buffalo
and cut the ham strings of both legs and the others
would come along and kill it. About fifteen squaws
went up to skin the buffaloes and get the meat.
Mother and I went with them. The squaws would
rip the animals down the back from the head to the
tail and then rip them down the belly and take off
the top half of the hide and cut all the meat on that
side from the bones. They would then tie ropes
to the feet of the buffaloes and turn them over with
their ponies, and do the other side the same. After
they got the meat home, they would slice it up in
thin pieces and hang it up to dry. When it was
about half dry they would take a piece at a time
and pound it between two rocks until it was very

soft, and then hang it up again until it was dry. The dried meat was put into a sack and the older it got the better it was. This is the way they did all of their buffalo meat. This meat was generally kept for use in the winter and during the general gatherings of the tribe. I know that we had about five hundred pounds of it when we got to the place where the tribe was to assemble. It was about the last of August when the tribe had all assembled in Deer Lodge Valley, now in Montana.

It was a great sight to see so many Indians together and to think I was all the white person within three hundred miles. I could not begin to count the wickiups that were strung up and down the small stream as far as I could see, and the whole country was covered with horses and dogs. As nearly as I could find out, there were about six thousand indians in this great camp, but there might have been more. When I asked the chief how many there were, he said there were so many that he could not count them.

Mother kept very close watch over me for fear that I would get hurt or lost among so many Indians, and when I went around to see what was going on, she was nearly always with me to take care of me. She told me that Pocatello's Indians were very bad and that they would steal me and take me away off and sell me to Indians that would eat me up. She scared me so badly that I stuck pretty close to her most of the time. The Indians would run horses and bet so heavily on the races that I saw one Indian win fifty head of ponies on one race. Two Indians were killed while racing their horses, and a squaw and her papoose were run over and the papoose was killed.

Some of Pocatello's Indians had several white scalps they had taken from some poor emigrants they had killed. I saw six of these scalpe. One was the scalp of a woman with red hair, one a girl's scalp with dark hair, and four were men's scalps, one with gray hair, the rest with dark hair. I cannot describe my feelings when I saw the red devils dancing around those scalps. It made me wish that I were home again herding sheep and livng on greens and lumpy-dick.

Washakie's Indians had a few Crow scalps, for at this time the Crows and Shoshones were at war with each other. I am pretty sure they had no white scalps, or if they had, they did not let me see them.

The Indians had great times dancing around the scalps. They would stick a small pole in the

ground and string the scalps on it and then dance
around them and sing and yell at the top of their
voices, and make the most horrible noises I ever
heard. The leaders of the different bands would
take the inside, then the warriors would circle
around them, then came the squaws and the children on the outside, and the noise they made would
shame a band of coyotes. I have seen five hundred
Indians at a time in this kind of dance, and they
would keep at it until I would get sick and tired of
it, but they thought they were having a high time,
and most of those who were not gambling or racing
horses would keep up this dancing and singing at
intervals for a week or more.

The time was drawing near when we were to
separate and I was glad of it. Some of Pocatello's
Indians started out a few days ahead of the rest of
his band. A day or two before we were to start my
horse got away and went off with some other horses,
and I slipped away from my mother and went after
him. I had not gone far until I met some Indians
hunting horses, who said they had not seen my
horse. I went on quite a ways further when an Indian came up to me and said that he had seen some
horses go over a ridge about a mile away, and if I
would get on his horse behind him he would take

me over and see if my horse was there. I got on behind him and we started, but when we got to the top of the hill I could not see any horses in sight, and after we got over the hill he started to ride fast. Then I began to get scared, for I thought of the man-eating Indians my mother had told me about, and I asked him to stop and let me get off, but he whipped his horse the harder and went the faster. Watching my chance, I jumped off and about broke my neck, but I got up and started back for camp as fast as I could run. He turned and came up to me and threw his lasso over me. After dragging me about ten rods, he stopped and hit me with his quirt and told me to get back on the horse or he would put an arrow through me. I cried and begged him to let me alone, but he made me get on again and started off as fast as his horse could go, but I noticed that he kept looking back every little while. Pretty soon he stopped and told me to get off. I jumped off, and as I did so he hit me such a lick over the head with his quirt that it made me see stars for a few minutes. Then he started off on a run, but after going about fifty yards he stopped, pulled his bow and arrow out of the quiver and started towards me as if he intended to put an arrow through me. He only came a few steps, then suddenly whirled his horse and away he went over the prairie. I soon saw what caused his hurry, for a short distance away were some Indians coming towards me as fast as they could travel. When they got to me they stopped, and one of them told me to get on behind him and he would take me to my mother. I climbed up mighty quick, and before we got to the wickiup I met my mother. She had come out to meet me and was crying. She lifted me from the horse and hugged me in great fashion. She said one of Pocatello's Indians was trying to steal me, and she never expected to see me again.

Some Indians happened to see me get on the horse behind the Indian and told my mother, and Washakie sent those Indians after me before we had a chance to get very far away. Mother stuck pretty close to me after that while we stopped in this place, but I had such a scare that I didn't go very far from the wickiup unless mother was with me. The chief told me never to go alone after my horse if he got away again, but to let him know and he would have him caught for me; that the Pocatello Indians wanted me and they would get me if they could and sell me for a great many ponies, and then it would be "goodby, Yagaiki," Yagaiki was my Indian name. For a long time after that I had to go to bed as soon as it began to get dark for my mother would not allow me out after night-fall.

The camp finally began to break up in earnest, as small bands started off in different directions, and they were about all gone when we started. There were about sixty wickiups and two hundred and fifty Indians in our band. We had about four hundred head of horses, and more than five hundred dogs, it seemed to me, all of them half breed coyotes. Chief Washakie was at that time about twenty-seven years old, a very large Indian, and quite good looking. His wife did not appear to be over twenty years old, and had one little boy papoose about six months old.

Pocatello was not as large as Washakie. He was a Shoshone, but his wife was a Bannock. She had three children when I first saw her. Pocatello was a sneaking and wicked looking Indian, and his tribe did more damage to the emigrants than any other tribe in the west. At that time he wanted to be chief of the Shoshones, for he thought he ought to be the leader because he was older than Washakie, but the tribe would not have it that way. He drew away about five hundred of the tribe, however, and wanted to change the name to Osasiba, but Washakie's Indians called them Saididig, which means ''dog stealers." When this band of outlaw Indians joined us in the Big Hole Basin, they had new quilts, women's clothes, and new guns, watches, saddles, and hats. Mother told me they had just attacked a large train of emigrants and had killed the people, burned their wagons, and had robbed them of everything they had. I saw some very large horses and a few mules with them. Mother wanted to buy from them a saddle and a hat for me, but I told her I would not use them; that I did not want to wear a hat whose owner had been killed and scalped by old Pocatello. Washakie and Pocatello were never very friendly. Pocatello wanted to kill and rob every white man that came his way, but Washakie wanted to be friendly with the white man, for he knew the Indian would finally get the worst of it. Because he thought it would be much better to live in peace than to fight, Pocatello called him a squaw, and said he was afraid to fight.

We got started from the big camp at last, and I was very glad of it for I was tired of being looked at by so many Indians. There were hundreds of young Indians in the big camp, and some old ones, too, who had never seen a white person before. They would gather around me like I was some wild animal. If I moved suddenly towards them, they

would jump back and scream like wild cats. My
mother told them I would not bite, but if they bothered me very much I might kick some of their ribs
loose, for I could kick worse than a wild horse.

We had not traveled more than two or three
hours before one of the horses turned his pack under
his belly and began to run and kick like mad. This
started all of the other horses, and as they came running by us, mother tried to stop them and one of the
horses ran against her and knocked her horse down
and it rolled over with her. I thought she was
killed. I jumped from my horse and raised her up
and then I saw that she was not dead, but that one
of her arms was broken. Washakie's wife was there
and told me to go ahead and tell Washakie to hurry
back. I think I never cried harder in my life than
I did then, for I thought my poor old mother was going to die. She told me not to cry, that she knew
she would be all right soon. We had to stop here
for a week to let mother get better. There were lots
of antelope in the valley and plenty of fish in the
stream by the camp, so when mother would go to
sleep, I would go fishing. I could tell every time
she woke up, for when Hanabi, the chief's wife,
came out and called, "Yagaiki, come," I knew that
mother was awake and had missed me. Then I

would get back to her in double quick time.

While we were waiting for my mother to get better, I went out with Washakie to see the Indians run antelope. About fifty of us circled around the antelope and would take turns in running them. It was not long until we had them run down. The poor, little animals became so tired that they would stick their heads under a bush and lie there until we had shot them with our bows and arrows. I killed two myself, and it tickled me nearly to death. When I got to camp I told mother how it all happened and she bragged on me so much, that I thought I was a heap big Indian. Well, mother's arm was doing nicely, for the medicine man had fixed it up pretty well.

We started again and traveled for several days, and then stopped where there were a great number of buffaloes and antelope. We stayed there for about three weeks. During the time that mother was not able to watch me, she had Washakie take me with him on his hunting trips, which just suited me. I went out with him to kill buffaloes, and the first day we killed six—two large bulls and four cows. One Indian, with a broad spear, would run up behind them and cut their ham strings so that they could not run and then we would go up and shoot them in the neck with arrows until we killed them; then the squaws would come and take the hide and meat and leave the bones. I told Washakie that my bow was too small to kill buffaloes with. He laughed and said I should have a bigger one.

When we got back to camp he told some of the Indians what I had said, and one very old Indian by the name of Morogonai gave me a fine bow and another Indian gave me eight good arrows. You bet, I felt big then, and I told mother that the next time I went out I would kill a whole herd of buffaloes. She said she knew I would, but that she did not know what they would do with all the meat. Washakie said I was just like the white men, they would kill all the buffaloes they could see and let them lie on the prairie for the wolves. He said it was not that way with the Indians, for they save all of the meat and hides. That the Great Spirit would not like it if they did as the white men; for they would have bad luck and would go hungry if they wasted meat and killed buffaloes and deer when they did not need to.

Two or three days after this we went out again and killed two more buffaloes. When we got back that night, mother asked how many I killed. I told her that I shot twice at them and I believe I hit one once. She said I was all right, and that I would be the best hunter in the whole tribe after a while. I told her that I would get a gun and then I would kill buffaloes for the whole band. She said I was a bully boy, and that I would be a chief some day. It took mother's arm a long time to get well and she suffered with it very much, but I was having a fine time and was getting fat. The bucks would kill the meat, but the squaws would have to carry it to camp and cook or dry it. They had to carry all the wood and the water. The men would lie around until they ran out of meat and then they would go out and hunt again.

CHAPTER V.

VILLAGE LIFE.

Cold weather was coming, for already some snow had fallen in the mountains. Hanabi and some of her friends went to work and made me some fine clothes. They were made somewhat like the shaps of the cowboys, open in front, with no seat, but on the sides wedge shaped strips that ran up to the belt. The leggings fit pretty tight, but the women left a seam about as wide as my hand on the outside so they could be let out if necessary. They gave me a pair of new moccasins that came up to my knees. They also made me another mother-hubbard out of nice, smoked buckskin, that fit me better than the first one did. The sleeves came down a little below my elbows, and had a long fringe on the outside from the shoulder down and all around the neck. The skirt part of the thing came down almost to my knees and had fringe all around the bottom of it, with beads in heart and diamond shapes all over the breast. The clothes were all very fine and when I got them on I couldn't tell whether I was a boy or a little squaw papoose. I didn't care much, either, for they fit me pretty well and were warm and comfortable. Mother made me a hat out of muskrat skin. It ran to a peak and had two rabbit tails sewed to the top for tassels. With my new clothes on, I was fixed up better than any other kid in the camp.

We now started for the elk country. When we got there the Indians killed about one hundred elk and a few bear, but by that time it was getting so cold that we set out again for our winter quarters. After traveling for several days we stopped on a large river which we called Paitapa, and which the whites call the Jefferson River, in Montana.

By this time, most of the buffaloes had left for their winter range, but we could see a few once in a while as they passed near our camp. The Indians did not bother them because we had plenty of dried meat and for fresh meat there were lots of white tail deer near the village that we could snare by hanging loops of rawhide over their trails. There were also a great many grouse and wild chickens. I have killed as high as six or seven a day with my bow and arrows.

Winter passed very slowly. Nothing very exciting happened until along towards spring when one day we had a terrible fracas. Washakie had gone up the river a few miles to visit another large Indian village to stay a day or two. While he was gone pretty nearly all the camp got into a fight. We had a fishing hole close to the camp where the squaws and kids would fish. Mother and I had been down there with a lot of others fishing through the ice, and had caught quite a nice lot of fish when mother took what we had to the wickiup. She told me not to stay long. As soon as she had gone, a girl, a little larger than I was, wanted to take my pole and fish in my hole. I let her take it, and she caught several fish. Then I heard mother call me and wanted her to give me back my pole, so I could go home, but she would not do it. I tried to take it away from her, but she jerked it away from me and hit me over the head with it and knocked me onto my knees. I jumped up and gave her a whack that knocked her down, and when she got up she gave a few of the awfulest yelps I ever heard. I did not know that one person could make so much noise as she did. Then she put for her home as fast as she could go, and knowing that something was likely to happen pretty quick, I gathered up what fish the kids hadn't run away with and went home, too. I was just inside our wickiup when the girl's mother came rushing up with a big knife in

her hand. She said: "Give me that little white
devil till I cut his heart out." She started for me,
but mother stopped her, pushed her back and got
her out of the wickiup.

They made such a racket that the whole camp
gathered around to see the fun. The squaw hit
mother over the head with the knife, and when I
saw the blood fly, I grabbed a big stick and struck
the squaw over the head and knocked her down.
Then I saw another squaw take hold of mother and
I sent her spinning. Then others mixed in and took
sides and soon the whole bunch was yelling and
fighting fit to kill. One boy grabbed the stick to
take it away from me, but I gave him a kick that
settled his hash. Hanabi took the stick away from
me and then I ran into the wickiup and got my bow
and arrows, but a big Indian took the bow away
from me and broke the string. If he had only left
me alone I would have made a few good squaws in
quick time. I guess it was for the best anyway.
More Indians came up and stopped the fracas, but
not before a lot of them went off howling with sore
heads. That night Washakie came home and they
held a big council. I don't know what they did, but
the next day two or three families left our camp
and went to join another band.

Everything passed along very well for a while. I helped mother pack wood and water, and the other little boys called me a squaw for doing it because carrying wood and water was squaw's work. I told mother I would break some of their darned necks if they didn't stop it. She said, "Let them alone, they are bad boys." But one day we were packing wood, and having cut more than we could carry in one trip I went back for it, when a boy came up to me and said, "Oh! you are a squaw," and spit at me. I threw down my wood and started after him. He ran and was yelping at every jump, expecting me to kick the top of his head off. Washakie happened to see me before I caught him and called to me to stop. It was lucky for that kid that Washakie was there, you bet, for if I had caught him I would have fixed him so that his mother would not have known him. I went back and got my wood and took it to the wickiup. Washakie wanted to know what it was all about, so I told him what the boy had called me and how he spit at me. He said he did not want me to start another camp fight, but that he did want me to take my own part, even if it caused the whole tribe to go to fighting. He said he had been watching how things were going, and was glad to say that so far

as he knew, 1 had never started a fuss and that he
did not think I was quarrelsome if I was let alone.
He said that if I was cowardly and afraid to stand
up for myself, the little boys would give me no peace
and so he was glad to see me take my own part.

One day I heard an Indian talking to Washakie
and telling him that it was not right for him to let
me do squaw's work, and that it was setting a bad
example for the other little boys. Washakie said
he thought it was setting a good example, and if
some of the older ones would take it, it would be
better for their wives. He said: "We burden our
women to death with hard labor. I have never
noticed it before so much as I have the last year
since we have had Yagaiki. I see how much he
helps mother and what lots of hard work she has
to do while we sit around and do nothing. Yagaiki
appears to be happier when helping mother than
he is when playing with the other little boys, and he
is so much comfort to her that I firmly believe
mother would have gone crazy if it had not been for
him. Her troubles were so great after my father
and my two brothers were killed, nearly at the same
time, that it was more than she could have stood.
I do believe it was the Great Spirit that sent the
little white boy to her."

I think if any thing had happened to me it would have killed my mother. She would say to Washakie: "You have no idea how smart that boy is. He asks me questions that I can hardly answer. One day he asked me why the Indians did not haul and cut the wood for their women. He said that was the way his father did for his mother. He said the Indians ought to pack the meat, too. If the women tanned the hides and made the clothes and moccasins for the family and did the cooking, it was their share of the work. He says the Indians ought to take care of their own horses or send their boys to do it, and that it is not right for the women to do all the work and let the men lie around doing nothing." I heard all this talk going on one night when they thought I was asleep. Washakie agreed with most of what his mother said, but of course, they couldn't change the Indian's way of doing things.

The warmer weather of spring had by this time melted some of the snow away, and as she came near she found the body of one of her boys partly uncovered and one of his feet had been eaten off by the wolves. She quickly dug the body out of the snow, and nearby she found her other boy. She was too weak to carry them back to her wickiup and she couldn't leave them there all night alone for the wolves. The next morning, Washakie found her lying on the snow beside the bodies of her children. He took them up tenderly and carried them back to the village, but the poor, old mother was very sick for a long time after that. She was just getting well when the band of Indians she was with came to the settlement where I lived and first saw me.

She would tell me about things that happened when she was a little girl. She said her father was a Shoshone and her mother a Bannock. She said she was sixty-two years old when I came, and had had four children, three boys and a girl. The girl was seven years old when she was dragged to death by a horse. Her oldest and youngest sons were killed in the snow slide, and Washakie and I were the only ones she had left. She had passed through many hard and sorrowful events in her life, but was having better times now than she ever had before, and if I would stay with her she knew she would be happy once more. She said she had fifteen head of horses of her own and when she died she wanted Washakie and me to divide them between us. She said she wanted me, when she died, to bury her like the white folks bury their dead, for she thought that way was the best.

CHAPTER VII.

THE CROWS.

The winter was breaking up and we commenced to get ready to move to the spring hunting grounds, but when we started to gather the horses we found that about fifty head were missing. After a while the Indians found the trail where they had been driven off by the Crow Indians. Our Indians followed them, but the Crows had so much the start that they could not overtake them, so we lost fifty head of our best horses. Mother lost six head, Washakie eleven head, and the rest belonged to the other Indians of the band. My little pinto was all right, for I had kept him near the camp with the horses that we used through the winter. Our Indians declared that they would make them all back before another winter. I found that was the way they would do. The Crows would steal every horse they could from the Shoshones, and our Indians would do the same with them, so I could not see that there was much harm done. It was as fair for one as it was for the other, and they would fight every time that they met. The Crows were always

on the watch and if they ran on to a small bunch
of Shoshones they would make it hot for them, and
the Shoshones would do the same to them, so there
was excitement and war dances going on all the
time.

We left our winter camp and started south.
After two days' travel, we came to another large
Indian camp and both camps kept together during
the rest of the summer. We traveled south for three
or four days and stopped where there was plenty
of all kinds of game, such as buffalo, elk, deer, and
antelope. We stayed here a few days, then went
east three days' travel and came to a beautiful
lake that was fairly alive with fish. Oh, how I did
catch them! There was plenty of game everywhere.
We could see buffaloes at any time and in any direction that we looked. I had great fun fishing
and running antelope. Washakie said I was riding
my horse too much, that he was getting poor, and
that I had better turn him out and he would give me
another. I was glad to do this for I knew my horse
was getting thin, and I wanted to give him a rest
and let him get fat. The horse that Washakie gave
me was a pretty roan, three years old, and partly
broke. When Washakie saw how well I managed
my new horse, he told me that I could break some
young horses for him to pay for the one he gave

me. That just suited me, for I did like to be around
wild horses. The horses were very small, especially the two-year-old colts which he wanted broke. I
wanted to get right at it, but he said I must wait
until they got fat so they could buck harder.

We were not far from the line that was in dispute between our Indians and the Crows. One day
some of the hunters came in scared nearly to death,
and said the Crows were coming right on to us.
I never saw such excitement in my life. Everybody
was running around and talking at the same time,
and the bucks were getting their war fixings on as
fast as they possibly could. The horses were rounded up and driven into camp, and you never saw
such a mixup in your life—horses, squaws, dogs, papooses and wickiups, all mixed together. The war
chief told all the young warriors to get out and meet
the Crows, and the old men to stay and guard the
camp. I said if I was going to fight, I wanted my
pinto; but mother said, "You are not going to
fight." I said, "I am." She said, "You are not, you
little fool, you can't fight anything." I said, "That
is what I came out here for." She said: "I will tell
you when to fight. You come and sit down by me;
I doubt if there is a Crow in five days' ride from
here. I have had too many such scares." I said,

"And aren't they coming?" She said, "Don't be afraid." I told her I was not afraid, that I would like to see the Crows and see if they had wings. I said the crows in our country all had wings. She said that the Crows were Indians like the Shoshones. By this time the squaws had everything packed up to put on their horses that were standing ready with their saddles on, and the old men had gathered in small bunches, all talking at the same time. It was not long until we saw the bucks coming back, and when they came up they said it was nothing but a herd of buffaloes running this way—no Crows at all. I began to think they were all cowards, the whole bunch of them. I was disappointed, for I hoped to see some fun.

Well, the next day about fifty of the young warriors left for some place, I could not find out where. Everything passed off in peace for a while. We fished and chased antelope, and one day I went with Washakie up in the mountains to kill elk. We had not gone far when we saw a large herd of elk lying down. We left our horses and crept up close to them. Washakie had a good gun, and his first shot hit a big cow elk. She ran about a minute and fell. Washakie told me to slip up and shoot her in the neck with my arrows until I killed her, then cut her throat so that she would bleed, and then stay there until he came back. Well, I crept up as close as I dared, and shot every arrow at her I had, and then climbed a tree. I guess she was dead before I shot her, but I did not know it, and I was too much afraid to go up to her. Washakie followed the herd that ran down the canyon.

I stayed up in the tree for about two hours, then came down softly and went up to the elk and threw sticks at her, but she didn't move. Then I thought she must be dead, so I went up to her and cut her throat; but she had been dead so long that she did not bleed a bit. I stayed around there a long time. After a while I began to get scared. I thought the bear would smell the elk and come and find me there and eat me up, so I started to where we left the horses, but I could not find them; then I started back to the elk, but I couldn't find it, either; then I did not know what to do. The timber was very thick and I was getting more scared all the time. I went back to where I thought the horses were and hunted all around, but I could not find them. By this time the sun had gone down and it was very dark and gloomy among the trees. I climbed another tree and waited a long time. I was afraid to call for fear of bringing the bear onto me.

Afterwards, I learned that I had not left the elk long until Washakie came and took the entrails out of it, and as he did not see my horse he thought I had gone on to camp. Before following the elk, he had tied my horse to a tree, but he had broken loose and gone off. When Washakie got to camp and found I was not there, and heard some of the Indians say they had seen my horse loose with the saddle on, he didn't know what to do, and mother almost went crazy. She started right out to hunt me, and about seventy-five Indians followed her. A little after dark, I heard the most awful noise. I thought sure the Crows were coming after me, but pretty soon I heard some one call my name, "Yagai-ki! Ya-gai-ki'!" Then I knew they were our Indians, so I answered him. Pretty soon I heard the brush cracking right under my tree, and he hallooed again. I said, "Here I am." He said, "What are you doing up there?" I told him I was looking for my horse. "Your horse is not up there." I said, "I know it." He told me to come down which I did in a hurry. He said: "Get on behind me, the whole tribe is looking for you, and your poor mother is nearly crazy about you. It would be better for her if some one would kill you, and I have a notion to do it. It would save her lots of trouble." When we got out of the timber he began to halloo just as loud as he could to let the rest know that I was found, then I could hear the Indians yelling all through the timber. He started for camp and when we got there, mother had not yet come in, so I was going back to look for her, but Hanabi would not let me go. She told me that I might miss her and get lost again; that I had given her enough trouble for one night. It was not long until mother came. She grabbed hold of me and said: "Yagaiki! Yagaiki! where have you been? I was afraid a big bear had got you." She talked and cried for almost an hour. She blamed Washakie for going off and leaving me alone. She said that I should never go with him again, that I must stay with her.

The next morning, as a squaw and mother and I were starting out to get the elk, Washakie asked me if I was sure I could find it. I told him I knew I could, so we started and I took them right to it. Mother said, "Where was it you were lost?" I said I was not lost, that I knew where camp was all the time. She said, "Why did you not come home, then?" I replied that I was waiting for Washakie to come, because he had told me to stay there until he came. "Well," she said, "you had better stay with me until you get a little older." I told her I liked to hunt, but she said I had lots of time and could go hunting another year. As we were skinning the elk, mother remarked that I had spoiled the skin by shooting it so full of holes. We got back to camp with our meat, and found it very fat and nice.

Everything went along all right during the next few days, and nothing happened worth speaking of until the Indians, that went off about ten days before got back. They had thirty-two head of the Crow's horses, but one of our Indians had been killed by the Crows. A young Indian that was with them told me about their raid. He said after they left camp they went over on the head of the Missouri river, which the Indians call Sogwobipa, where they found a small band of Crow Indians, but the Crows had seen them first and were ready for them. He said they saw a bunch of horses and watched them until after dark. Then they started to get the horses and just before getting to them, they were met by a shower of arrows and a few bullets which killed one of their party, and wounded five or six of their horses. One of the horses was so badly crippled that he could not travel so the rider jumped onto the dead Indian's horse, and they all broke back as fast the their horses could carry them with one hundred Crows after them. They were chased by the Crows all night, but they finally made their escape.

A few days after this, as they were going through a range of mountains, they came suddenly upon a small band of the Crows, killed two of them, and took all their horses. They thought the whole tribe of Crows was following them, so they cut a line for home. I thought it was pretty tough for about fifty to jump on a few like that, rob them, and leave them without horses. I think Washakie didn't like it, either. I told him it was not fair. He said it was too bad, but the Crows would treat us that way, but it was not right for either to do it. Well, the Indians were quite uneasy, for they thought the Crows would follow them up and be on us at any minute, so we kept a strong guard out all the time.

Washakie thought it best to get a little further from the line and in a more open country so they could watch their horses better. They did not appear to value their own lives so much as they did their horses. I asked Washakie why it wouldn't be better for the chiefs to get together, talk the matter over and fix things up and stop this stealing from one another. He laughed and said that when I got

a little older I might fix things up to suit me, but as
things were going now, he had to be rather careful;
that Pocatello had poisoned the minds of many of
his tribe and drew them off, and that he could not
do just as he wanted to, but if he could, there would
not be any more fighting.

The camp packed up and made a start for the
open country, and there was a long string of us.
We traveled south, down the river from this beautiful lake, for about seven days and came to another large stream that came from the east, and
when the two came together it made a very large
river, which the Indians called Piupa. We put our
wickiups by a small stream that came out of the
north fork of this big river. It was not very wide,
but quite deep, and was full of fish. What fun I
had catching them! After we had been here a few
days, Washakie said that when I was ready I could
start in to breaking the colts. That was just what
suited me, so we caught one, tied it to a tree and
let it stand there until it stopped pulling back, then
it would lead. We let it stand there all day and
at night he helped me to lead it to water. Then
we staked it near camp and let it eat there all night.

The next morning I found I could lead it to
water alone, so I thought I would try to ride him.

I was putting my saddle on him, but mother said to ride him bareback. I told her I could not stick to him without my saddle. She said, "Well, do as you like"; so I went to work to saddle him, but he objected to that, and came nearly getting away from me. Mother said, "Tie this old blanket over his head so he can't see." I fastened him to a bush, and threw the blanket over his head, and mother came and helped me tie it on. By this time about fifty kids had gathered around to see the fun. Well, I got my saddle on him and mother said, "Now you get on and I will pull the blanket off." I got on and said, "Let him go." Off came the blanket and away went the horse. He whirled and sprang in the air, and came down with his head between his front legs. I went flying towards the creek and didn't stop until I got to the bottom of it. When I crawled out and wiped the water out of my eyes, I could see the colt going across the prairïe, with the saddle under his belly, and kicking at every jump. Mother said, "Let him go." I said I would ride that horse if I never killed another Indian. She said, "How many did you ever kill?" I said that the number that I had killed was nothing to what I was going to kill, and I had a notion to start in on some of these black imps now if they did not look out and quit laughing.

When I got some dry clothes on a young Indian came up on a horse and I got him to go and catch the colt for me. When he brought him in, he helped me tie a strap around him as tight as we could get it, just so I could put my fingers under it, then he held the colt while I got on him. When I said, "Let him go," Mr. Colt started off on a run, and the young Indian followed after me and kept the colt out of the brush and away from the other horses that were staked around. The colt soon got tired and stopped running. I had a fine ride. The Indian boy stayed with me until the colt got tired, then we took him to camp, and I staked him out. It took mother and me two days to gather up my saddle, and when we got it all it was in such a bad fix that we could hardly tell what it had been in the first place. It took us about a week to fix it up again, but we made it a great deal stouter than it was. The next day I rode the colt again and I soon had him broke. The next colt was not so bad for me to ride, and I soon got so I could ride any of them without much trouble.

About this time we had another stampede. One night the Indians thought the Crows were on us sure, for one of the guard came running in and said he had seen a big band of Crows coming. It was in the middle of the night, but all the squaws and papooses were pulled out of bed and told to get into the brush and stay there until morning. I told mother that I would not go one step without my horse. She said that I could not find him in the dark, but I said I could for I knew right where he was. I started for the horse and mother started after me, but I outran her. I could hear her calling, "Yagaiki! Yagaiki! kamy, Yagaiki! kamy!" I happened to find my pinto and jumped on to his back, and was at my mother's side in a few minutes. She said, "You little fool, the Crows might have got you." I said, "There are no Crows in a thousand miles of us." She said, "How do you know?" I said I would have to see them before I would believe they were coming. Well, the Indians gathered up all the horses and stayed around them all night. Mother and I and Hanabi went down the river about a mile where there were seven or eight hundred squaws and papooses scattered through the willows. They made such a noise that nobody could sleep, for they thought they would all be killed before morning.

Well, morning came and no Crows. The Indians were all as mad as hornets, or at least they all acted that way. Washakie sent out a few men to where the guard said he saw the Crows, and when they got back they said there were no signs of Indians, but that the guard saw a big dust, and thought it was the Crows coming. I told Washakie that guard ought to be killed, that if a white man had done such a thing he would have been put in prison for ten years. I told him I had got so that I could not believe any of them but him. He said it was a shame, but they would do that way and he could not help it. I asked him how he could tell when the Crows were really coming. He said he had a few good, trusty men, and when he thought there was much danger he would send out some of these, or would go himself. I asked him if he thought there was any danger of the Crows coming to attack us. He said he did not look for them to come to fight at this place, but that they might watch around to try to steal our horses, and if they could run on to a few of our men out a little way from camp, they might kill them.

Everything went on quietly again for a while. I kept on breaking colts and whipping kids every once in a while. One day I was out riding a wild colt and there was a lot of boys along with me. Among them was a boy that I had kicked in the head for trying to raise my mother-hubbard to see my sore legs, when I first came to live with the Indians. He had a long stick and would punch my colt with it every time he got a chance. At last I said, "See here, young man, what do you mean by jabbing my horse?" He said that he wanted to make him throw me off for kicking him that time. I said, "Now, look here, if I get another kick at you, I will break your darned, black neck." Pretty soon he jabbed my horse again. I had a long rawhide rope tied around my colt's neck. I took the other end and made a noose in it and when he punched my horse the next time, I threw the noose over his head and jerked him off his pony. That scared my colt and he broke and ran. Before I could stop him, I had nearly choked the life out of that kid. The blood was coming out of his nose and mouth, and I thought I had surely killed him. As soon as I loosened the noose though, I found he could squall in good shape, and when he got up he started for camp, lickety split, and at every step he groaned as bad as a dying calf.

I started for camp, too, for I knew that hell would be popping very soon. He went past our wickiup and mother asked him who hurt him. He said, "Yagaiki." Before I got home I met mother.

She said, "Yagaiki, what have you been doing?"
I said, "Trying to kill a blamed kid." "Well, you
have come very nearly doing it this time. How
did it happen?" I told her all about it. She said,
"It will cause another camp fight." "I don't
care," I said, but I really did care a great deal. I
turned loose the colt I was riding and started after
my pinto pony. She said, "Where are you going?"
I said, "After my horse." "What for?" she
asked. "Because I want him," I said. When I
had caught and saddled him, I saw the boy and
his father and mother and a few more coming, so
I jumped on my horse and started off. Mother
called for me to stop, but I didn't stop. I thought
if they wanted to fight, they could fight; I did
not want to fight, so I got out of it as fast as pinto
could carry me. I went up the river and hid in
the brush. About dark, I could hear Indians calling,
"Yagaiki!" but I did not answer them.

After a while the mosquitoes got so bad in the
brush that I could not stay there, so when everything was still I crept out, but then did not know
where to go or what to do, so I sat down on a stump
and tried to think what was best for me to do. I
knew there would be a racket in camp over what
I had done, and I hated it like everything on ac-

count of mother. I was not a bit sorry for the kid,
and I felt then as if I wouldn't have cared much
if I had killed him. I had some pretty tough feelings as I sat there on the stump. I was more homesick just then than I had ever been before. I was
so far from home, and with a lot of Indians who
were mad at me. I did not know but what they
would burn me as soon as they got hold of me. I
felt pretty bad, and these lines that I had heard
my sister sing came to my mind:

"Oh! pity the fate of a poor young stranger
That has wandered far from his home;
He sighs for protection from Indians and danger,
And knows not which way to roam."

Well, after thinking the matter over, I decided
it would be better for me to go back and face the
music, let it be what it would. When I got near
the camp I met a lot of Indians that mother had
sent to hunt me. When I saw them I stopped and
they came running up to me and said, "Yagaiki,
we are hunting you." "What for?" I asked. They
said that my mother had sent them, and they asked
me if I had seen Washakie. They said that he was
out hunting for me. When I asked them what the
Indians would do to me, they said they would do
nothing to me, that I had done just what any

one else would have done. I said I was afraid it was going to start another fight, but they laughed and said it would not. This made me feel much better. When I got to camp and mother saw me, she said, "Yagaiki, where have you been?" When I told her, she said I was the most foolish boy she ever saw for running off like that. "Well," I said, "I thought if I went away it might keep down another fight in camp." It was not long until Washakie came in, and he gave me a long talk. He said for me never to run off that way any more, that when I got into trouble, to come to him and he would see that I was not hurt. I told him I had better go home, for I was always getting into trouble and making it hard for mother and him. He said he would not let me go home for that, but that I must be a little more careful, for I might have killed the boy if I had not stopped just when I did. He said a rope tied to a wild horse and around a boy's neck hasn't much fun in it for the boy. I told him I did not think about the rope being tied to the horse or I would not have done it, but the boy made me so mad I did not know what I was doing. I told him the boy was doing all he could to make the horse throw me off, and if he ever did it again I would wring his blasted neck off. He told me the boy's neck was much skinned, and his father and mother felt very badly about it, but he would talk to them and try to fix it up. The other little boys that were with us said I did just right. Washakie had a long talk with the boy's parents and I heard no more about it, but I saw the boy going around with a greasy rag around his neck, and when he came around where I was he would look very savagely at me.

The mosquitoes got so bad at this place that we had to move. We went east nearly to the Teton Peaks, where we found all kinds of game plentiful and the streams full of trout. We came to a beautiful valley with a river running north and south through the center of it. There was no timber growing on its banks, but there were great patches of willows from one to one and one-half miles wide extending for about twenty miles up and down the river. The white-tailed deer were plentiful among the willows. I killed five while we were there and mother tanned the skins and made a suit of clothes for me out of their hides. The clothes were quite nice and warm. There were also a number of moose killed among the willows.

Washakie told me that his tribe had a great fight with the Sioux Indians in this valley many years ago when he was a small boy, and that his people lost about two thousand of their best men. He took me all over the battle ground.

We stayed in this valley about thirty days and I started to breaking more colts. When I got up the first one after our racket, mother said, "Leave your rope here." I told her that I could not do without it. "Well, don't use it on any more kids," she said. Everything passed off here very quietly except for two or three scares the Indians had when they thought the Crows were after them. If they saw a dust made by the wind they would send out to see what caused it. They were like a band of sheep that had been run by wolves. Every little thing would scare them. It made me tired to see them so cowardly. I told Washakie that I did not think they would fight if they had a chance. I said, "When are you going to send more Indians out to steal the Crows' horses?" He said, "Why, do you want to go with them?" I said, "Not much, I have not lost any horses." "Well, we have," he said, "but I have nothing to do with that kind of business, the War Chief attends to all that. If the Crows do not come after us we will send out a party against them after a while, but I do not know just when. We must, though, get back the horses we have lost, and do it before the snow comes." I asked him if he was going to winter here in this valley. "Oh, no, the snow falls too deep here. After the buffalo get fat and we get what meat we want for our winter use, we will go west, a long way off, to winter where no buffalo run, but where there are plenty of deer and antelope and fine fishing." He said that some of those fish were as long as I was.

The Indians killed a great many elk, deer, and moose, and the women had all they could do tanning the hides and drying the meat. Berries were getting ripe so we would go up in the mountains and gather them to dry. I had lots of fun going with mother to gather the berries. One day while we were up in a deep canyon we found plenty of berries and were busy gathering them, when all at once we heard some awful screaming. Pretty soon here came a lot of squaws and papooses. "Wudutsi nia baititsi ke kudjawaia. Wudutsi!" one said. That means, "A bear has killed my girl." I jumped onto my pinto, for I was riding him that day, and started up through the brush as fast as I could go. When I got a little way up the canyon, the brush was not quite so thick, and I could see a bear running up the hill. I went a little further and found the girl stretched out on the ground as if she were dead. Then I yelled as loud as I could for some of the Indians to come back, but they had all gone. I tried to lift her onto the horse, but she was too heavy for me, so I laid her down again. Then she asked for a drink. I took the cup she was picking berries in and gave her some water. I asked her if she felt better. She said, "Yes, where is my mother?" I said they all went down the canyon like a lot of scared sheep, and that they must be nearly home by this time. Seeing that she felt better, I took her by the arm and helped her up.

She was crying all the time and said her head and her side hurt her very much and that her arm hurt her, too. I asked her if she could ride. She said she would try, so I helped her on to the horse and led it about three miles until we got out of the canyon, then she said, "You get on behind, I think I can guide the horse." So I got on behind her, for we had to go about four miles yet to reach camp. When we got in sight of camp, we saw some Indians coming full tilt, and when we met them there was the greatest hubbub I ever heard. When we got to camp, her mother came running up and threw her arms around the girl and hugged and kissed her, and cried and went on like she was crazy. She would have hugged me, too, if I had been willing. She said I was a brave boy. Mother came up to me and said, "Yagaiki, I thought you had come down to camp ahead of me, or I never would have come without you." I said, "You were as scared as any of them." She said, "I know I was scared, but I never would have left you if I had known that you had not come out of the canyon."

That night the girl's mother and father came to our wickiup to see what I wanted for saving their daughter's life. I told them that I wanted nothing for doing what I ought to do. Her father said, "You are a good boy, and a brave boy, too." I asked her mother why she ran off, and left the girl behind in that way. "Well," she said, "I saw the bear knock her down and jump on her, and I thought she was dead, and that if I went up to her the bear would kill me, too; then there would be two of us dead." Her father said the way so many got killed by bears was because, if a bear caught one, others would run in and get killed. He said it was best if one got caught by a bear for the rest to run and get away while the bear was killing that one. I said that I did not like that way of doing, that I thought if a bear got hold of one, the rest should go after the bear and kill it, and that I would try to save anyone that got caught by a bear, even if I got killed myself. "I know you would, my brave boy. You have already shown what you would do," said my mother. Washakie said: "Don't brag on the boy too much or you will make him think he is a hero. Well, it was a brave act in the boy, and he will be more thought of by everybody in the tribe after this." Mother said that I would be one of the greatest war chiefs the tribe ever had when I got to be a man. She said she always knew there was something about me that was more than common. Washakie said, "Well, that is all right, let us go to sleep." The girl's mother told me that I could have her daughter for a wife when I got big enough, but I told her she could keep the girl for I did not want her. She said, "Maybe you will change your mind when you get older." The next day, I wanted mother and a lot more Indians to go up the same canyon to gather some more service berries. "No, sir," they said, "you don't get us up that place any more after berries." The thoughts of the bear scared them nearly to death. The Indians did not have much to do with bears, but if they came across one out of the brush in open ground, they would sometimes attack him.

One morning we saw two bears crossing the valley, and about fifty Indians on horses started after them. I ran and got Pinto, and when I came for my saddle mother said, "Where are you going?" "I am going to help kill those bears." "What bears?" "Those bears going yonder." "You are not." When Washakie told her to let me go, she consented, so I jumped on to the horse and started after the bears as fast as I could peg it. The Indians had headed them off from the timber and were popping arrows to them in good style. My horse was not a bit scared of them, so I ran up pretty close to one of the bears and put three arrows into his side. The Indians said, "Keep back, you little fool, that bear will tear you to pieces." But Mr. Bear was too full of arrows to tear much, for by this time you could hardly see him for arrows. He looked like a porcupine with the quills sticking out all over him. We soon killed the two bears, but the skins were so full of holes that they were not worth much, and the meat wasn't much good, either. That night they had a big dance around the two hides, and would have me join them and sing as loud as any of them, for they said I was the most daring one among them. One old Indian said, "The little fool don't know any better.

If a bear ever got hold of him he would not be so brave." Anyhow, they gave me the best hide. Mother tanned it and sewed up most of the holes, and it made a very good robe for me to sleep on.

Another small band of Indians came to our camp and the girl that hit me with the fishing pole was with them. After she saw that the Indians were so kind to me, and liked me so much, she wanted to make up with me. She came around several times before she said anything to me, but finally, one day, she came to where I was helping mother stake down a moose hide so it would dry, and said, "Yagaiki, I am sorry that I hit you that day with your fish pole." I said, "I am not." She said, "Why?" I said, "Because we had lots of fun that day." Mother said, "Yagaiki, why don't you make up with her?" I said I did not want to; that I would rather give her a few more kicks. "Kiss her, you mean boy," said my mother. Well, I didn't kiss her, but I told her it was all right, that we would be friends again. She said, "Good! Come to our wickiup some day and play with me." "Not much," I said, "your mother will cut my head off with that big knife she has, if I go near her." "No, she will not hurt you. She is coming over to make it all right with your mother. She is very sorry

for what we did to your folks, and so is my father.''
Well, everything was fixed up and we became pretty
good friends after that.

By this time we had gathered all the berries
that grew along the foot hills, for the squaws were
afraid to go up into the mountains after the bear
excitement. They also went to work in dead earnest
in tanning the elk and deer skins, and in drying
meat for use during the coming winter. The Indians had quit hunting for elk and deer for they
had all the skins that the women could get ready
to take to some trading post where they could be
swapped for red blankets and beads and other Indian goods. About every fall they would go to Salt
Lake City to sell their buckskins and buffalo robes.
Mother and Hanabi worked all day and away into
the night to get their skins ready in time, and I
helped them all I could. I took an old horse of
mother's, went to the foot hills and snaked down
enough wood to last while we were there. I packed
all the water for them, too, and no kid dared to
call me a squaw, either.

Well, the time had come for us to start killing
buffaloes for the winter supply of meat. We did
not have to hunt them, either, for we could see them
at any time, and in almost any direction. Many

a time I would go with Washakie to see the Indians
kill the buffaloes. Washakie only wanted five, and
we soon got them; but it would take mother and
Hanabi many days to tan their hides for market,
and dry the meat for winter use.

CHAPTER VIII.

A LONG JOURNEY.

Nothing went wrong while we were getting ready for the long trip to market, and finally everything was in shape to pack up. Our camp was very large by this time for Indians had been coming in every few days, until they numbered over a thousand, and there must have been all of five thousand horses. When we got ready and started, I could not see half of the long string of pack horses. We had for our family twenty pack horses loaded with buffalo robes, and elk and deer skins, besides our camp outfit. Washakie had a fine, big wickiup of elk hides, made so it would shed rain. It could be divided into two parts, and sometimes we would put up only half of it, if we were going to stop one night, but if we were going to stay for some time, we would put it all up.

After we got started, I noticed that the Indians broke up into small bands. That night there were about twenty-five wickiups left in our camp, but I could see many other camps scattered up and down the river. Washakie said that it was better to travel in small parties, for we could get along faster, and the horses could get better pasture and would not be so much bother. In two or three days we got to the Big River where I had come near choking the boy to death with my rope. It was quite wide and the current was very swift where we forded it. When we got in the deepest place, mother's horse stumbled over a cobble stone and fell, and away went mother down the stream, for it was so swift that she could not withstand the current. I saw her going and started after her, but I could not catch her until she was carried down into deep water. My horse was a good swimmer, so I was soon at her side. I pulled her to the bank and helped her out of the water. By this time we were quite a distance down the stream where the willows were very thick, and we had a hard time getting out. We soon met Washakie coming to help us. When he came up he said, "Mother, you came nearly going to the happy hunting grounds that time." "Yes," she said, "but I have someone with me to help me in time of need. I am not afraid of anything when Yagaiki is with me." Washakie thought we had better camp there so mother could put on dry clothes and get over her scare, for he was afraid it would make her sick.

That night we camped in a grove of cottonwoods near the river, and just before dark an Indian came running in and told Washakie that the Crows had overtaken a small bunch of the tribe, had killed them, and taken all their horses. Washakie told the war chief to take every one of our Indians and follow them even to the Crow country if he had to. The war chief told his men to get ready for a long trip, and the women and children to hide in the willows until they heard from him. I never saw such excitement among the squaws and kids in my life as we had there. Mother said, "Come on, Yagaiki, let us get to the brush." "Not by a d——n sight," I said. "I am going with the warriors to kill Crows." Mother got me by one arm and Hanabi by the other, and mother began to cry and said to Washakie, "Make him come." Washakie laughed and said that I was just fooling, that I had not lost any Crows, and that I would go with them. He said he was going to guard the camp. "So am I," I said. Mother said, "I want you to guard me and Hanabi." Washakie said, "Go with them and see that nothing hurts them." I ran out, caught Pinto, put my saddle and a few buffalo robes on him, and mother and Hanabi and I started down the river.

When we got down to where the rest of the crowd was, and I could hear the kids howliing like young coyotes, I said, "What is the use of hiding when there is such a noise as this going on? If the Crows have any ears they can hear this noise for five miles." Mother said that made no difference, for the Crows didn't dare to come into the brush after them. I asked her if the Crows were as big cowards as our crowd. She said they were. I said, "There is no danger, then, so we had better go to sleep." It was not long before we heard Washakie call for us to come to camp. "There," I said, "another scare is over with no Crows at all. I will never hide again." When we got to camp I learned that a few Crows had chased some of our Indians and had fired a few shots at them, but nobody had been killed, and not even a horse had been stolen. About fifty of our young warriors were following the Crows, but I knew they would never overtake them.

The next day we packed up early and hit the trail pretty hard, and for several days we headed south. We left the large river that the Indians called Piupa, crossed over the mountains, and came to a place they called Tosaibi, which I learned later to be Soda Springs, in the southeastern part of Idaho. We could not use the water of the springs, so we went a short distance and camped on a large river which the Indians called Titsapa. They said this river ran into a big salt lake that reached nearly to my old home. That started me to thinking of home and my dear mother, brothers, and sisters that I would like to see so well, and I could feel the hot tears running down my cheek. Mother saw them and came and sat down by my side and said, "Ya-gaiki, I fear you do not like to live with us." I said, "Why?" "What are you crying about?" she asked. I told her that I was thinking of my white mother. She said, "Am I not as good to you as your own mother?" I told her that she was.

We went down this river one day's travel, and there we stayed three days. From here part of our band was going to take the buffalo robes and buck-skins and what furs we had to Salt Lake City to sell them. I wanted to go with this party, but mother would not let me. Hanabi and Washakie took twelve pack horses very heavily loaded and also two young horses to sell if he got a chance. They left mother and me with the camp outfit and sixty-four head of horses to look after. Those that were not going to Salt Lake City intended to go off northwest and strike the head of another river which was about four days' travel from where we were, and stay there until the others returned.

Well, Washakie and the rest of them started on their long journey to the big city of the white people. When mother and I went to pack up to go back we found we did not have pack saddles enough for all of our camp outfit. We had sixteen sacks of dried meat, two sacks of service berries, and all of our camp outfit and only eight pack saddles. Mother said we could get along if we had two more saddles. I told her that if my saddle would do for one to take it, for I could ride bareback. She said it would, but she did not like to take it. She did take it, however, and another boy let us have his saddle, so we packed up ten horses. You see we could not get off very early in the morning for, although it did not take long to pack one horse, it took quite a while to pack ten of them. There were fifteen squaws, about thirty-five children, and three old Indians in our camp. After traveling three days we came to the head of the river which they called Tobitapa, but which is called now by the white man, the Portneuf river.

Washakie thought it would take them fifteen days to go to Salt Lake City and get back to where we were. I asked mother if she was not afraid the Crows would come and kill the whole lot of us while the others were gone. She said, ''No, the Crows never come this far south." I asked her why she did not want to go to Salt Lake City with the others. She said we had too many horses, and that she was afraid the white men would take me away from her. I asked her if that was the reason that Washakie did not like to have me go with him. She told me that Washakie said if I ever got dissatisfied and wanted to go home he would give me my horse and fix me up in good shape, and send two Indians with me to see that I got home safe. "But," she said, "I hope you will never want to go away from me, for I believe it would kill me now if you should go away and leave me." I told her I thought I never would want to leave her. I could see that she always seemed happier when I would tell her that I would always stay with her. She would do anything to make me happy. If she ever saw me look unhappy, I could see that she would turn away and cry.

She was afraid that I would get sick by not having bread and milk to eat, for I had told her that I always had bread and milk for supper when I was at home, so she thought that eating all meat would not agree with me and would make me unhealthy. She would often have fried fish and fried chickens or ducks for supper, but she would not let

me eat any of it if she could help it. When I first
went to live with her she made a small sack and tied
it to my saddle and would keep it full of the best
dried fish, so that when we were traveling, I could
eat if I got hungry, for she said I could not go all
day without eating anything as the Indians did.
Every morning she would empty my sack and fill it
anew so that I could eat all the time if I wanted to.
She soon found out what I liked best and she always had it for me, so you see I always had plenty
to eat, even if I was with the Indians, and that is
more than a great many white children had at
home.

I was very healthy while I was with the Indians.
I guess the reason was that I did not like the way
they doctored. When any of them got a cold or was
sick, they would dig a hole two or three feet deep
by the side of a cold spring and put in a few cobble-
stones. Then they would build a fire in the hole,
get the stones right hot, and then scrape the fire all
out. The sick person had to get into the hole with
a cup of water, and after the hole was covered with
a buffalo robe, he would pour the water on the hot
rocks and make a steam. This would soon make him
sweat like sixty; and when he had sweat long
enough, someone would jerk the robe off the hole,

and he would jump into the cold water of the spring. As soon as he got out of the water they would throw a buffalo robe around him, put him to bed, and let him sweat a while, then they would cool him off gradually by taking the cover off a little at a time until he quit sweating. He was then thought to be well.

One cold, chilly day I was out hunting chickens and was quite a distance from camp when a heavy rainstorm came up and soaked me through and through before I could get home. That night I coughed all night so that nobody could sleep. The next day mother wanted to dig a hole for me. I told her not much, that I did not want a hole dug for me until I was dead. She begged me to take a sweat. I told her she would not get me to jump into any more springs like they did when I had sore legs. She said it would not hurt me. I told her that was played out, I would not do it. She said, "Well, you need not jump into the water, the heat of the ground, and the steam from the rocks will sweat you enough," and asked if I would do that. Washakie said, "Yes, do it and get well before you are down sick in bed." I said, "Go to digging." She soon had the hole dug and everything ready; then she said, "Come on now, pull off your clothes and get in here." I said, "Pull off nothing." She said,

"You must." Washakie said, "Jerk them off, I will hold this buffalo robe over you so you will not be seen." They got me to pull off my clothes and get into the hole over the hot rocks, just like an old sitting hen does over her eggs, and mother gave me some water to pour on the rocks. She stood there to keep the robe over the hole, and would keep asking me if I was sweating. I told her that I was getting wetter than a fish, but for some cause she kept me there for quite a while, until I begged pretty hard to be let out, then she jerked off the robe and shewhack came three or four buckets of cold water all over me. Oh, gosh! didn't I get out of that hole quick! Washakie stood there with the robe, threw it over me, carried me into the wickiup and put me to bed. He threw more robes over me and I lay there and sweat like a horse. This was after Washakie and his party had got back from Salt Lake, but they were gone twenty-two days instead of fifteen.

Snow had already fallen on the tops of the mountains when Washakie got back, so he was in a hurry to get the camp moved to the winter range, and mother and Hanabi began at once to arrange the packs for traveling. Washakie had disposed of his robes and skins at a good price, and he had sold the two horses, so he came back pretty well fixed.

He had twenty-four red blankets, and a lot of calico, some red flannel for the tongues of moccasins and two pairs of drawers for me, and about a peck of beads of all colors and sizes. The beads were to swap for tanned buckskin and the blankets for buffalo robes. He brought me a butcher knife, a new bridle, two pounds of candy, and a lot of fish hooks.

We soon started for our winter quarters. We went down the Tobitapa (Portneuf) to the Piupa (Snake River), then up the Piupa, and then over the divide on to the headwaters of Angatipa (Rock Creek). At this place we stayed six days and killed sixteen buffaloes, two for each family. That was to be the last killing of buffaloes until the next year. Washakie bought four of the buffalo hides, which made him six in all. He said he wanted something for the women to do through the winter. When we started from here, we went west over a big mountain upon which we had to camp in about three feet of snow. We had to tie up all our horses to keep them from running away, for we had nothing for them to eat. We were off pretty early the next morning, and that night we got out of the snow, but it was still very cold. The next day we came to a beautiful stream. It was not very large, but it was fairly alive with mountain trout. We went down this stream two days' travel, and there we stayed

for about a month, I think. When we stopped
Washakie intended to stay there during the winter,
but afterwards he changed his mind and we went
down the stream until we came to another large
stream. I do not remember what the Indians called
this river, but they told me that fish as long as I
was came up that river in the spring.

We had a very good camping ground that winter.
It was sheltered from the wind, but we had a great
deal more snow than we had the winter before.
About six hundred yards above our camp was a
large grove of dry quakingasp, which was pretty
much all small poles. I told mother that if she
would help me pile a lot, I would haul them down
for her with the horses. She did not believe I could
do it. But I got her to help me make a big pile of
the poles. She said she knew we would have to
pack it if we got it down to camp. Washakie had
brought from Salt Lake City the inch auger I asked
him to get for me, so I went to work to make a sled
like I had seen my father make. I got two crooked
sticks for runners, pinned on some cross pieces, and
soon had the thing made. It did not look much
like a sled, but it answered the purpose pretty well.
I got up two lazy old horses of mother's, put on
their pack saddles, and tied ropes from the sled to
the pack saddles. I got on one of the horses and

away we went for the grove. I put on quite a few sticks, tied them with a rope, and took the load to camp without any bother at all. All of the Indians and squaws and papooses were out watching me bring in my first load of wood. The old war chief said, "What cannot a white man do?" In a few days I had all of the wood down to camp. Hanabi said I was as good as two squaws.

After I got my wood down I loaned my sled to some of the Indians. They thought they could haul wood as well as I could, so they hooked up two horses like I had done and started for the grove. They went up a little higher than I did, where it was quite a bit steeper than where I got my wood. They put on a big load and started down; the sled ran into the horses' heels, scared them, and they started to run. The one the Indian was riding broke loose from the sled, but the other horse ran with the sled fastened to him, scattered the wood all over the side of the hill, and came bolting down through the camp. The sled jammed against the wickiups and jerked three or four of them down. Then the frightened horse struck out through some cottonwoods, slammed the sled against the trees and broke it all to pieces. This discouraged the Indians and they said the squaws could pack the wood if they wanted any, that it was their work anyhow. That ended the wood hauling.

I got some of the Indian boys to help me fix up the sled again. We pulled it up on a hill with a horse and turned it towards camp. I wanted some of the boys to get on with me and slide down, but they were afraid to. They said that they wanted to see me do it first, so away I went down all right. They came down with the horse and we pulled the sled up again, and by hard begging, I got two of the boys on the sled with me. As soon as we started, one jumped off, but the other stayed on with me. When we reached the bottom, he said it was the finest ride he ever had. The next time several other boys said they would like to try it, and five got on. Away we went to the bottom. Oh, what fun we had! It was not long until they all wanted to get on, and the heavier it was loaded the faster it would go, and when the track was slick it would go nearly to the camp. We kept this up for days. When the track got well broke, we would pull the sled up ourselves without a horse. All the big boys and girls would join us in our coasting, and sometimes the older ones would ride, too. We kept the sled going all the time, until we wore the runners out, then we passed the rest of the winter in fishing and in hunting chickens and rabbits. Sometimes we would go for antelope, but when we went for them some of the older Indians would go along with us to keep us from killing too many.

Everything went off very peaceably this winter. There was no quarreling or fighting. One young papoose died and one old squaw did the same thing. We lost no horses. I had a real good time, and mother seemed to enjoy the winter as well as I did. We were a long ways from the Crows, so we had no Crow scares. Along towards spring seven or eight of us little boys were in the cottonwoods shooting birds, when one boy's arrow hit the side of a tree, glanced, and struck me in the leg. He was scared, for he thought I was going to kick him to pieces. I told the boy to stop crying, that I knew it was an accident, and was not done on purpose. He quit crying, and the other boys thought I was getting to be a pretty good fellow after all, for before this they believed that if anybody hurt me, there would be a kicking scrape right away.

Spring came at last. We moved down the river about fifteen miles where we could get better grass for our horses. Here were plenty of white tailed deer and antelope, some elk, and a few mountain sheep; ducks and geese were plentiful. We stayed here until about the middle of May. The big fish that they told me about began to come up the river, and they were big, too. Two of them were all I could carry. They must have weighed at least thirty or thirty-five pounds each. Mother and Hanabi dried about two hundred pounds of these fish, which I afterwards learned were salmon. The first that came up were fat and very good, but they kept coming thicker and thicker until they were so poor they were not fit to eat.

We started to move camp again. We went down the river a little farther, and then up a very deep and rocky canyon where there had been many snow slides during the winter. We crossed over snow that had come down in these slides that was forty or fifty feet deep, and as hard as ice. There was not much timber in the canyon, and the cliffs were very high. Years afterwards very rich gold mines were found in this canyon, great quartz mills were built, and a big mining camp was started.

As we left this canyon, we climbed a very steep mountain for about two miles, and then went down through thick timber, until we came out onto a beautiful prairie covered with the finest grass I ever saw. Off to the left was a deep canyon where one fork of the Big Hole River headed, and we camped here for a long time. Antelope and black tailed deer were plentiful, and we killed a great many of them and dried the meat. I think Washakie and I killed seventeen while we stayed here.

From this place we went down to the forks of the river, and I think we stayed there two or three weeks to give the women time to tan the deer skins. It was fine fishing in the Big Hole River. While we were staying here one of the war chief's boys was shot accidentally and killed. Oh! what crying we had to do. Every one in camp who could raise a yelp, had to cry for about five days. I had to mingle my gentle voice with the rest of the mourners. They killed three horses and buried them and his bow and arrows with him. The horses were for him to ride to the happy hunting grounds. When they got ready to bury him, every one in camp had to go up to him and put a hand on his head and say he was sorry to have him leave us. When it came my turn, I went into my wickiup and would not come out. Mother came after me. I told her I would not go, that I was not sorry to see him go, but was glad of it, for he was no good anyhow. Mother said, "Don't say that so they will hear it." Then she went back and told them I was afraid of dead folks and she could not get me to come, but that I was in the wickiup crying fit to break my heart.

They took him to a high cliff of rocks and put him in a crevice with his bedding, a frying pan, an ax, his bow and arrows, and some dried buffalo meat, and then covered him up with rocks. When they got back to camp they let out the most pitiful howls I ever heard. I got down to it, too, just as loud as I could scream. Could you have seen me, you would have thought I was the most broken hearted one in the whole camp. I got so hoarse I could hardly talk. When I was doing my best howling, I had to get behind a tree once in a while, or get in the brush where nobody could see me, for I would have to stop and laugh half of the time. Well, we kept this up for five days—a little every day. I did feel sorry for his poor mother. She cut her hair off close to her head. I asked mother why she did it. She said that all the mothers did it when their oldest boy died.

After our mourning came to an end, we moved down the Big Hole River to where the town of Melrose is now. Plenty of game was to be seen everywhere. The bitter weeping had ceased, except that of the poor mother, whose mourning could be heard for a mile. We stayed here about two weeks, then went down the Big Hole River until it emptied into the Beaver Head River, and formed the Jefferson River. We did not do anything here but fish, for the buffalo were not fat enough to kill, and besides, we had all the dried elk and deer meat we wanted. It was a beautiful place to camp, and we had the finest grass for our horses. I broke a few more colts —two for mother and four for Washakie. By this time our horses were getting fat and looking fine, but my little Pinto was the prettiest one of all. Hardly a day passed but what some Indian would try to trade me out of him. One Indian offered me two good horses for him, but I thought too much of him to swap him for a whole band of horses. He was just as pretty as a horse could be.

Our next journey took us a long ways northeast. Washakie said we would go to where the buffaloes were too many to count. We traveled for a week and came to the north fork of the Madsen River, about on a line with the Yellowstone National Park, and oh! the kwaditsi (antelope), and padahia (elk), and kotea (buffalo), were in great herds. Everywhere that we might look we could see them. While we were at this camp, another boy was killed by a horse. When I heard of it, I told mother to get her voice ready and her throat fixed for an-

other big time, and that I was going to do my best
for him, but it would not be because I felt very
sorry. Hanabi said, "Yagaiki, aren't you ashamed
to talk that way?" and mother said she was afraid
that I was a hard-hearted boy. Well, we all turned
out and gathered up all the pieces of him we could
find, for the horse had dragged him through down
timber and over rocks, and when he stopped running there was not much left of the boy.

From there we went up the Madison River
about ninety miles, where we stayed a month. The
buffalo were getting fat, so we killed quite a few
and dried the meat and made their hides into robes.
Then we went on south and came to a beautiful
lake where we had such a good time the summer before. This lake is now called Henry's Lake, and
is the head of the north fork of the Snake River. We
did nothing here but fish, for we had dried meat to
last until we got to the usual hunting grounds.

CHAPTER IX.

THE FIERCE BATTLE.

We were now traveling towards the Crow country, and I think our Indians were a little afraid that the Crows were going to try to stop them if they could; but Washakie said he was going through if half his tribe were killed, for he was not going to be bluffed off his best hunting ground any longer. I thought something was up, for small bunches of Indians were coming in all the time, and we had gathered a very large band of us, until we numbered about seven hundred warriors. We sent all of our surplus horses down the Snake River with Indians to guard them until we came back. Washakie and mother kept fifteen head for pack horses, and I kept my two horses to ride. After the extra horses and packs had gone, we started for the disputed hunting grounds.

The men all went out ahead, followed by the pack horses, with the women and children and the old men in the rear. Mother said I was to keep close to her, for Washakie said the Crows might tackle us that day. I said that kind of talk was too

thin. But we hadn't been traveling very long before one of the three or four Indians that had been
sent on ahead came tearing back and said that he
had seen where a very large band of Crows had
passed, and that he saw a smoke in the timber
ahead. The men all stopped and bunched up. I
heard Washakie tell them to go ahead and keep
a good lookout, and if the Crows jumped onto them,
to fight as long as there was a man left. I thought
they must be getting brave. Well, we started again
with the men on ahead of us as before, but riding
very slowly. Six or eight Indians were riding back
and forth to keep the squaws and pack horses from
getting scattered. Pretty soon we stopped again,
and the war chief said: "We will camp here for tonight. We know now that we must fight or go back,
and we have done that so much that the Crows begin to think we are afraid of them; but I feel that
we ought to give them a lesson this time that they
will not forget soon." Washakie said, "That is the
way I look at it. Now is the time to show them
that we will fight for our rights." This seemed to be
the way most of the warriors felt, for I heard them
talking about it in their council that night.

Well, we camped right there all in a bunch,
and hardly had room to make down our beds. A

"Uncle Nick" Leaving Home to go with the Indians on His Pinto Pony

strong guard was sent out to look after the horses, but the night passed off without any trouble, and when morning came, ten men were sent to see if they could find any signs of the Crows. They were gone about an hour when back they came, and said that about a thousand Crows were camped over the ridge just ahead of us. The war chief said, "We shall go on to the hunting grounds, if there are ten thousand of them."

The Indians painted up in grand style. They drew black streaks all over their faces to make themselves look fiercer, and then we got ready and started forward. We had not gone far, when the squaws were ordered to stop, but the warriors went on and passed over a small ridge out of our sight. Pretty soon we heard shooting, and an Indian came and told us to go back until we came to good water, and to stay there until we heard from the chief. He said, "They are fighting now." We had hardly reached the stream of water, before we saw the Indians come up on the hill and then disappear, and then come in sight again. We could see that they were fighting very hard, and we could hear them yelling to beat Old Billy. They had not been fighting over an hour before half or two-thirds of them were on top of the hill and slowly coming down the side towards us. The squaws began to cry and said the Crows were getting the best of our Indians and were driving them back. They kept coming closer and closer to us. When I looked around I saw that all the squaws were getting butcher knives and were ready to fight if they had to. Then I noticed that our men were not coming towards us any longer. I could see Washakie on his big buckskin horse riding around among his Indians and telling them what to do, and pretty soon they began to disappear over the ridge again and I could tell then that our Indians were getting the best of the Crows.

We could tell the Crow Indians from ours for they had something white over one shoulder and around under one arm, and they wore white feathers in their hair. There were about fifteen hundred Indians engaged in the fight on both sides, so you can know that the battle ground covered quite a piece of country. We could see lots of horses running around without riders. I believe that many of the squaws would have taken part in the battle if it had not been for the guard of about fifty old Indians that rode around us all the time to keep the squaws and the horses close together. I could see plainly now that our side was driving the Crows back. When they had driven the Crows back to the ridge, they seemed to stick there, but were still fighting and yelling and circling round and round. It looked as though they could not drive the enemy any further. I got so excited that I jumped on my horse and said to another little Indian boy, "Come, let us go up there and see what they are doing and try to help them." Mother grabbed my horse by the bridle and said, "You crazy little fool, haven't you got one bit of sense?" I said, "I might kill a whole flock of Crows for all you know." After they had been fighting about six hours, one Indian came back, very badly wounded, and told us to go back to the lake, but not to unpack until we got word from the war chief. We went back and when we got on top of the divide we could see the Indians fighting, although they were about two miles away, and we could see loose horses all over the prairie. We reached the lake when the sun was about an hour high. About dark half of our Indians came to us and the war chief said to unpack and put up the wickiups for very likely we would stay there for a while. He told us that about sundown the Crows broke and ran, and that Washakie with the other half of our Indians was following them to try to head them off and keep them from getting away. Washakie thought that he and his warriors could stop them until morning and then the whole of his band would attack them again. The war chief sent twenty Indians with one hundred fresh horses to overtake our Indians that were following the Crows, for their horses had been on the go all day and were about worn out. He said he saw twenty-five of our Indians that were dead, and he did not know how many more had been killed. An Indian asked mother if she had any horses she could let them have to take back. She said she had two they could take, and I said they could take my roan pony. We had the horses staked close by and soon had them for him.

By this time three or four hundred squaws and papooses were wailing and moaning in such good shape that you could have heard them for two miles. I asked mother when our turn would come. Hanabi said, "Do hush and go to sleep." But there was not much sleep that night. When day came I never saw such a sight in my life. About two hundred Indians had been brought in during the night, all very badly wounded. I went around with mother to see them. One poor fellow has his nose shot off and one eye shot out, and he said that he did not feel very well himself. Many of them were so badly hurt that I knew they could not live until sundown, and I thought about half of them would die that day. A few old Indians were sent over to the battle field to keep the eagles and wolves from eating the Indians that had been killed. The war chief had been shot in the arm and in the leg, but was not very badly hurt. He had gone before I got up that morning, and had taken with him all the warriors that were able to go.

Well, that night a little after dark all of our Indians came back. Washakie said the Crows had gone into the thick timber so that he could not get them out, but that there were not many of them left anyhow. Our men brought in a very large band of the Crow's horses and saddles, and when they were unpacked, I never before saw such a pile of buffalo robes, blankets, bows and arrows, and guns.

The next morning we all started out for the battle ground to bury the dead, and, oh! what a sight! There were Indians scattered everywhere, all over the battlefield, and oh! what pitiful wails the squaws and papooses made when they saw the dead Indians lying around. Wives were hunting among the dead for their husbands, and mothers were looking for their sons. I went around picking up arrows. I had gathered quite a few when mother saw me with them. She said, "Throw them down, quick. The old Indians will come around to gather them. Don't touch anything.'' I said, ''What do they want with them?'' She said that they would keep them until another fight. The squaws scalped every Crow they could find. I saw mother scalping one and I said, ''Aren't you going to scalp our Indians?'' She said, ''No!'' I said, ''You ought to scalp them and send the scalps to the Crows, for they killed them and ought to have the scalps.'' She said, ''Go off. You don't know what you are talking about.'' Our Indians carried our dead to a deep washout in the side of the hill, put them in and covered them with dirt and rocks. The dead Crows were left to the wolves and buzzards. That night, when I got back to camp, I was very tired and hungry, and I had seen so many Indians scalped that I felt sick and wished from the bottom of my heart that I was home with my kindred.

About two hundred and fifty horses were captured from the Crows. We had thirty-one Indians killed, and three hundred wounded in the battle. Eighteen of the wounded died afterwards, which made forty-nine that we lost in this terrible fight. Washakie sent out a few of our men to count the Crows that had been killed, and when they got back they said they found one hundred and three dead Crows, and Washakie said that about that many more were badly wounded and would die. That would make over two hundred killed on the Crow side, and forty-nine on our side. I began to change my mind about our Indians being cowards after seeing that fight. I have seen many a hard fight between white men and Indians, and only in one of them did I see greater bravery than was shown by our Indians in that great battle. We had to stay here about three weeks on account of our wounded.

By the time the wounded could be moved, it was too late for us to go the rounds Washakie had planned, so we thought we had better get ready for winter. We moved camp over to the Angatimpa and started to kill buffaloes and dry the meat. We split up into small bands again. The Indians had quite a few widows to kill buffaloes for, and they had to go to market with the robes and skins, and it was getting late in the fall. The worst of it was that the man who was the best to cut the ham strings of the buffaloes had been killed in the battle, so we could not get along as fast with our hunting. However, we soon got all the buffaloes we wanted, and now the hides were to be made into robes. Poor old mother and Hanabi worked very

hard to get them ready so they could be sent to
Salt Lake with the crowd that was going.

Washakie had a good many buffalo robes. Besides what he got from hunting, he had bought
quite a number, and a lot had been captured from
the Crows, so he had sixteen horses packed with
nothing but buffalo robes and buckskins. We had
six packs of dried meat, and the camp outfit made
three more. We were, therefore, so heavily loaded
that we could not travel very fast. When we got
over the divide, Washakie said that mother and I
had better stop there with some of the others to take
care of the extra horses. I did not like to do this,
for I wanted to go to Salt Lake this time, but I
would do anything Washakie said. He told us we
could come on slowly after they got started.

When they started for Salt Lake they took with
them about thirty head of the Crows' horses to
swap for anything they could get for them. After
they were gone, there were about one hundred of us
left behind, mostly squaws and papooses and old
and wounded Indians, to take care of, and six hundred head of horses.

CHAPTER X.

LIVELY TIMES.

After the party had been gone two days, the balance of us moved down the creek to where it sank in the sand hills. Here three of the wounded Indians got so bad that we had to stop for some time, but we had the finest grass for the horses, and the sage-chickens were as thick as could be.

One day I was out shooting chickens and had killed four with arrows and was coming home, when, as I was passing a wickiup, a dog jumped out and got me by the leg and tore off quite a lot of flesh. I shot him through with an arrow, leaving the feathers on one side of him and the spike sticking out on the other. As I was trying to catch the dog to get my arrow back, the old squaw who owned him ran up with a rope and, throwing it over my head, jerked me along to her wickiup. She held me there while her girl tied my feet and hands, and then she got a butcher knife and was going to cut my head off.

A sick Indian who happened to be lying nearby, jumped up and held the squaw while a little boy ran and told mother. Mother came in double quick time and took the knife away from the squaw. She cut the strap they had me tied with, took me by the arm, and made me hike for my wickiup. When she saw my leg where the dog had bitten me, oh! how mad she got. She went back to the squaw and said, "If you do not kill that dog before sundown, I will kill you." I had followed mother. "Look here," she said, "and see this poor boy with his leg nearly bitten off." The old Indians that had gathered around stopped the fracas, or I guess there would have been another camp fight.

Mother went for the medicine man. When he came he said it was a very bad bite, and that we would have to be careful or blood poison would set in. He said the dog would have to be killed. I said I thought the dog would die if they would let him alone; but he said, "The dog must be killed before he dies." That almost made me laugh. The cut in my leg was "V" shaped, and the piece of flesh hung only by the skin. When he went to put it back in place I said, "Ouch!" He asked, "What did you say?" I said, "Ouch!" "What is that?" I said I did not know. He said, "Oh!" He put the piece back in place and stuck it there with something, then he got some weeds, mashed them up and made a poultice and put it on the wound.

He said he would go and have the dog killed. I told him he would have to hurry up or the dog would be dead. "When I have had the dog killed I will come back and put another poultice on your leg," he said. I asked, "What are you going to put two poultices on for?" He replied that he intended to take that one off and put a fresh one on. I said, "Oh!"

Now, when the medicine man told anyone to do anything he had to do it. He sent a big boy to kill the dog, and when the boy got to the wickiup the old squaw and her girl pitched onto him and beat the poor fellow nearly to death. Then the medicine man sent two big Indians to see what they could do. When they reached the place, I could hear very loud talking, so I got up and went to the door to see the fun. One Indian had hold of the old squaw and the other had the girl, and they were shaking them for all that was out. I said, "Go after them, old boys." Mother said, "Shut your mouth and come in here and lie down." I told her I wanted to see the squaw and her girl get a good shaking. Well, they killed the dog before he died, anyway.

When everything was again quiet in camp, the medicine man came and changed the poultice on my leg. It had swollen very badly by this time. He told mother to boil sage leaves, and with the tea to bathe my leg very often. I could hear mother crying while she was gathering the sage, and when she came in I asked her what she was crying about. She said she was afraid I would be lame all my life from the hurt. I told her I would be well in a week; that a little thing like that would not make me lame very long. My leg pained me so that I did not get much sleep that night.

The next morning the squaw and her girl and their wickiup were gone, but the sick Indian was left lying there alone in his bed. I told mother to let him come into our wickiup and stay until his squaw got back. She had gone with Washakie to sell her robes and skins and had left her wounded husband with her sister-in-law to take care of until she got back. Mother did not like to take him in until I told her that he had saved my life by keeping the old squaw from cutting my head off, then she went out and told him to come into our wickiup and stay until his wife got back.

The poor fellow was very sick, and so weak that he could hardly walk. He had been shot three times with arrows—in the arm, in the leg, and in his side. His side was the worst. The medicine man had to take out a part of two ribs, and the hole left was big enough for me to stick my fist in. It kept the medicine man busy to tend to me and all of the wounded Indians. Mother bathed my sore leg three times a day with the sage tea, and the swelling all went away, and I was getting along fine. In about a week I had mother get me some sticks and I made some crutches, then I could get around out of doors. When the others that were lame saw how well I could move about they had me make them some crutches so they could get out, too.

After staying here about two weeks we had to move, for the wood was getting scarce near camp. I hobbled around and helped mother pack up, and we went over through the sand hills and came to a good sized stream, which they called Tonobipa. This stream ran south through the sand hills and lava beds, and the Indians told me that down farther it sank out of sight into the ground.

The sick Indians had a very hard time of it while we were on the move, but I stood it very well. We could not stop at this place very long, for we had to go to the place where we were to meet Washakie. That was five days' travel away, so we only stopped here four days, then we started on again. One day we had to make a twenty-mile drive to reach water. We could not travel very fast because of the sick Indians, and we could not get started very early in the morning on account of having so many horses to pack, and I was not much help to mother. It seemed an awful long ways until we got to Piupa.

That day was too hard on our sick Indians, and we had to leave two of them in the sand hills and go on until we came to water, and oh! how tired I got, and how my leg did hurt me. When we left the two Indians, one old Indian started ahead to get them some water and bring back to them. Well, it was away after dark when we got to the river, and you bet I was glad to get a good drink of water, and lie down to rest awhile. My leg hurt me so much that mother would not let me help her do a thing. She unpacked all of the horses and put up the wickiup alone.

The medicine man came to fix my leg, and when he unwrapped it to put on a poultice he found it had turned black. He said that it had begun to mortify and would have to be cut off. Then mother began to cry so that the whole camp heard her, and a lot of the Indians came up to see what was the matter. She told them that her poor boy had to have his leg cut off. I said, "Not by a d——n sight." I told the old medicine man to pike away to his wickiup and not to come back any more. Mother cried and begged the medicine man not to go. She said I was out of my head, and did not know what I was saying. "Yes, he does," said the old rascal, "and I do not care if the little, white devil does die." I said, "I know you don't, or you would not want to cut my leg off." I said that I knew very well what I was saying, and I wanted him to get, and get quick, too, and that when Washakie came I would see that all of his legs were cut off. Away he went, as mad as fire.

After he had gone, mother said, "Now you have run the medicine man off, you will die." I said, "Not half as quick as I will if he keeps putting his poisoned poultices on my leg." I said that I would have been well long ago if it had not been for him, and that the old fool did not know as much as a last year's bird's nest with the bottom out; that I knew he had been trying to kill me ever since he began to doctor me, and I was not going to let him do anything for me any more.

Mother gathered more sage and bathed my leg. The poor old woman worked with me nearly all night, and the next morning my leg was better, but I could not move it without a great deal of pain. Mother said she would not leave that place until I got well, even if we had to stay there all winter. A couple of squaws brought in the two Indians we had left in the sand hills the night before. The next morning, when mother got up, she said she dreamed that Washakie came and killed a sage-hen and put the entrails on my leg and it cured it right away. I told her to keep on with the sage tea, and I thought it would be all right in a few days.

After we had been here two or three days, some of the Indians wanted to go to the place where we were to meet Washakie and the crowd that was with him, but mother said she would move not one peg until I got better, so five wickiups stayed with us and the rest went on. When they reached the place they found Washakie and his party there waiting for us. When they told him how I was, he started out that night, and in two days he got to us. When he saw my leg and was told about it, he was very angry, and said it was bad enough to be bitten by the dog without having the squaw threaten to cut my head off. He said she would have to leave the tribe.

When I told him that every time the wound started to heal the old medicine man would squeeze it and break it open again, and that he nearly killed me every time he put the poultice on, he was very mad and said he would fix him when we got down to where we were going to winter. He said he had left his things in a bad shape, and would like to get back as soon as I could be moved. I said I thought I could travel, so the next morning we all packed up for the start. When I went to get on my horse, it hurt my leg so that I began to cry. Washakie said, "Hold on, I will fix you so you can ride better than that way." Then he and some more Indians went to work and tied some wickiup poles on each side of two horses, and then wove some rope between the poles. A lot of buffalo robes were thrown on, and this made a fine bed. Mother led the front horse, and away we went in first-class style.

After we got started, Washakie came up and asked me if they were traveling too fast for me. I said, "No, you can run if you want to," He laughed and said I was all right. As we went along that day mother got some boys to shoot some sage-chickens for her. The boys killed three and brought them to her, and when we camped that night she put the entrails on my sore leg. Oh, how well I slept that night!—the first good sleep I had had for more than a week. As we traveled along, mother took good care of my leg in this way, and by the time we got to the main camp, I could walk again with my crutches.

The next morning after we arrived here Washakie told the War Chief to send down the river for the best medicine man in the tribe. I told Washakie I would not let any more of his medicine men fool with my leg. He said he only wanted him to see it. That day the good doctor came, and when he looked at it he shook his head and said it was a wonder I was alive, for the old medicine man had been putting poison weeds on it, and if he had kept it up two days longer I would have been dead now. Washakie sent for the old medicine man, and when he came, said to him, "What have you been doing to this boy?" He said he had been doing all he could for me. Washakie said: "I don't want any more of your lies. Let me tell you that you have been making poultices out of poison weeds and putting them on his leg, and you have squeezed it until you can see the prints of your fingers yet. If this boy had died I would have had you tied to the tail of a wild horse and let him kick you to death and drag you until not one bit of meat was left on your bones. Now go, and don't let me see you any more,

for you are hated by every Indian, squaw, and papoose in this camp.'' We stopped here about two
weeks, and my leg got so much better that we moved
down the river to where we were going to stop for
the winter. Here fishing was good, and white tail
deer, sage-hens, ducks, and rabbits were very
plentiful.

CHAPTER XI.

OLD MOROGONAI.

During the time that I was disabled and had to stay in the wickiup, my old friend, Morogonai, would come and talk to me for hours. He told me all about the first white men that he ever saw. Lewis and Clark, he said, were the two chiefs, and they had about thirty-five white men with them. He said he sold them some horses and they were good, honest, white men. He said he traveled with them for ten days, and would catch fish and swap them for shirts.

He said he had nothing against the white men only that they had spoiled his country, and he believed that in a few years there would be no buffaloes, and the elk would all be gone, so that the Indians would have a hard time to get something to eat. He said before any white men came to this country they had plenty of game of all kinds. "We hear," he said, 'that away east of us the white men are killing the buffaloes by the thousands, and only taking the best of the skins and leaving all the meat to the wolves and the buzzards.'' He said that some of the white men that traveled through the country used their squaws very badly and had also brought diseases among the Indians that had killed many of them.

He told about an emigrant train that was on its way to Oregon, and while they were camped at the Humboldt Springs some of Pocatello's Indians went to their camp to swap buckskins for flour. The white men took three of their squaws and drove the rest of the Indians off. That made the Indians mad, so they gathered a lot more Indians and followed the white men and killed every one of them and took everything they had and burned their wagons. There were eighteen men and no women in the train.

He said that the men who carried the mail from Salt Lake to California would steal horses from the emigrants and take them to the Indians to herd, and when the emigrants were gone they would come and get the horses. He said: "I know this to be too true, for at one time these same men stole some very fine, big horses from a large train that was going through to Oregon, and brought them to my camp to keep for two moons, and then they were coming to get them and give us fifteen new red blankets for keeping them.

"In a few days, the emigrants found the tracks of their horses and following them up found the horses around our camp, and thinking we had stolen them, they let in to shooting without giving us a chance to explain. Well, they killed seven of my men before we knew what was up, and took their horses and some of ours. I was away at the time with most of our men. When I got back to camp, I found my oldest boy and five more Indians dead. One more died that night. Well, we got what was left of our band together and followed the white men for eight days before we could get a chance to do anything, for there was a good many of them and they kept a strong guard around their camp at night. But on the eighth day it was very stormy, and we stampeded their horses and got away with twenty-two head of them. The whites followed us and would have overtaken us had it not been that we happened to run into a large camp of Pocatello's Indians. We did not stop, but kept right on, and when the emigrants saw this camp, they thought these were the Indians that had stolen their horses. They had a big fight and men were killed on both sides, but the Indians finally got the worst of it. The best of it was, that we got away with the horses.

"After we got back to the main tribe, Washakie came to hear of it, and he sent for me and made me tell him all about it. When he heard the story, he said he did not blame me, but it was a bad scrape and he did not want any of his tribe to get into trouble with the whites. He said I had better keep away from the road where the white men travel, and not have anything to do with them, for they have crooked tongues, and no one can believe what they say.

"We did not know what the whooping cough, measles, and smallpox were until the whites brought these diseases among us. A train of emigrants once camped near my band and some of their children had the whooping cough and gave it to our children. Our Medicine Men tried to cure it like they would a bad cold, and over half of our children died with it. Hundreds of our people have died with the smallpox, and we lay it all to the white man.

"The white men keep crowding the Indians that are east of here west, and they keep crowding us west, and they will soon have us away out in Nevada where there is nothing but lizards, snakes, and horned toads; and if they crowd us any further, we will have to jump off into the great water."

He told me of so many low-down, dishonest

things that the white men had done to the Indians that I am ashamed to write it all in this book. Now, I believe that every word he told me is true. Now, my dear friends, I am glad to have you know that there is an Indian side to the tales of the early days in the "Great West."

When poor, old Morogonai was telling me his pitiful tales, I did not know how to sympathize with him then as I do now. Since I have seen so many bloody fights between the white men and the Indians, and being pretty well acquainted with both sides, I find that I cannot blame the Indians as some folks do. I know that they are a treacherous people, and revengeful, and if a white man kills an Indian, the Indians want to kill a white man to pay for it, and more than one if they can.

Nearing the Hunting Grounds

CHAPTER XII.

THE BIG COUNCIL.

Our winter camp was in a very beautiful place with plenty of game and lots of good, dry wood and nearly everything that was needed to make one happy. My leg and all the sick Indians got well, and we were having a fine time.

One day some of Pocatello's Indians came to our camp, and that night Washakie called a council of the tribe to meet at the war chief's wickiup. I thought this strange, for he always held his councils in our wickiup. The next morning they held another council, so I thought I would go and see what was going on. When I got to the door of the council wickiup, I met an Indian who told me to run back, that they did not want me there. I thought that funny, for I had never before been sent away from their councils. When I got back to our wickiup I found mother and Hanabi both crying. I knew then that something was up, but I did not know what, and they would not tell me a word about it. I thought Pocatello's Indians wanted Washakie to help them out in some bloody affair with the whites.

This ran along for four days, and I could not find out anything. I saw other squaws come to our wickiup and talk to mother, but when I came up they would stop talking, so I began to think it must be something about me, and it bothered me quite a little.

On the fifth morning Washakie sent for me and when I got there, I found about fifteen Indians gathered for the council. The war chief asked me how old I was. I told him I was nearly fourteen years old. He asked how old I was when I ran away from home. I told him I was nearly twelve years old then. He asked me if I was stolen away from home, or if I came of my own accord. I told him that I ran away from home; that nobody forced me to come, but two Indians coaxed me and gave me my pinto pony. Then he told me I could go. When I got back to the wickiup, mother and Hanabi wanted to know what they said to me and I told them all about it.

That night they held their council in Washakie's wickiup and the war chief asked me how long I had been with the Indians, how they had treated me, and why I ran away from home. I told him I had been with them two years, that I had been treated as well by the Indians as I ever had been at home, and that I ran away because I did not want to herd sheep all alone. I said the only way I could get the little pinto pony was to come with the Indians; and besides, they told me if I would come I would be treated well and would have plenty to eat and wear, so I came. The war chief asked if they had done as they said they would. I told him they had done everything they said they would do, and that I was not finding any fault. Washakie spoke up and said: "I told the Indians to offer the horse to the boy if he would come of his own accord. So when he came, we gave the squaw who owned the pinto, four colts for him. I gave her one yearling, mother gave her two, and Morogonai gave one. We never told the boy he could have the horse, but we knew the horse belonged to him all the same. I gave him another pony more to get him used to riding wild horses. He broke several colts for me and some for mother, and now he can ride anything in the shape of horseflesh."

The war chief asked me if I would rather live with the white people or with the Indians. I told him I would sooner live with the Indians. Then the council broke up and all the Indians went to their wickiups. I told Washakie I would like to know what it all meant. He said I would know in the morning. I told him if I thought they were going to take my pinto away from me, I would skip out that night with him. "They are not going to take your horse away from you. Wherever you go, that horse goes, too," said my mother. We all went to bed that night wondering what was going to happen in the morning. It was a very long night for me, for I did not sleep much.

Morning came at last, and after breakfast the war chief and a lot more Indians came to our wickiup and with them were those Pocatello Indians. When they all got into the wickiup, Washakie told me that these Indians had been down to where my people lived; that my father said I had been stolen by the Indians; that he was raising a big army to come and get me; and that he was going to kill every Indian he could find. Washakie asked me what I thought of that. I told him it was not so. "In the first place, my people do not want to fight the Indians; and another thing, if my father had been coming after me, he would have come long before this. I don't believe one word of it," I said. Washakie said he looked at it just as I did.

Then one of Pocatello's Indians said he had just come from Salt Lake City and lots of folks asked him if he knew anything of the boy that had been stolen from the white folks. He said that all through the white people's towns they were fixing to fight, and he knew very well they were coming after me. I said I knew they were not, for I heard my father say many times that if ever one of his boys ran away he could never come back again. "Besides, my father has an old Gosiute Indian living with him that knows all about my running away." Washakie said that he could hardly believe they were coming after me. "It doesn't look reasonable to me," he said, "that they would let this run so long, and then come to hunt the boy at this time of the year, and I don't think they will do it."

This made the Pocatello Indians mad and they said, "If you believe that white boy before you believe us, you can do it; and if you get into a fight with the white men, you need not ask us to help you." Washakie said he was not going to get into any trouble with the white people if he could help it. They said, "No, you are too big a coward to fight anything." Then they got up and strutted off. As they went out they said to one of our Indians that they would like to get that little white devil out in the brush and they would have another white, curly-headed scalp to dance around when they got back to their camp.

When the council met that night, it was plain that they did not have very much to say. They all appeared to be in a deep study. After a little while Washakie said he had been thinking that it would be a good thing to send some of our Indians down among the white settlements to see for themselves what was going on. Old Morogonai said it was the best thing that could be done, but "Who will go?" Washakie said it would not be hard to get enough to go. The war chief said he thought it would be better for the boy to go himself, for that would end all the trouble, and if his folks were after him it would stop them and settle all disputes. Nearly the whole council thought this was the best thing that could be done. Washakie asked me how I thought that would do. I replied that I did not know the way home and I would not go. He said if the council thought it best for me to go, they would find a way for me to get home safe. He asked each member of the council to say what he thought about it, and all of them said they thought it was the best thing that could be done.

Mother talked and cried a great deal. I do not remember all she said, but I know that she begged them to send somebody else. Washakie was silent a long time, then he said I had better go; that he would send two of his best men with me to the nearest white people's town, and then I could get on to my home myself. He said: "I want you to go home, and when you get there, tell the truth. Tell your father that you came with us on your own accord; and then, if you want to come back, we will be glad to have you come and live with us forever." I said, "All right, I will go home if you want me to, but I will not stay there." How mother did take on! It did seem as though it would break her poor, old heart; and Hanabi took it very hard, too. I told them not to feel bad, for I would soon be back.

In a few days I was to start for home, so we commenced getting ready for the journey. Hanabi and some more squaws went to work to fix me up in first class style, and in two or three days they had all my clothes made. The Indians gave me so many buffalo robes and buckskins that one horse could not carry them, and Washakie said I might have one of the horses that they had captured from the Crows. When the two Indians that were going with me said they were ready, we packed up. I had in my pack seven buffalo robes, fifteen large buckskins, and ten pairs of very fine moccasins. It was quite bulky, but was not very heavy. Just as I was leaving, the little boys gave me so many arrows that I could not get them all in my quiver.

CHAPTER XIII.

HOMEWARD BOUND.

When we started to leave the village, how my mother did cry! I tried to comfort her by telling her not to cry, for I would soon be back. Little did I think it would be the last time I would ever see her, for I felt certain that I would come back that fall.

We took with us plenty of dried buffalo meat to last us through the trip, and away we went. On the fourth day, at noon, we came to a place on the Bear River about twenty miles north of Brigham City, Utah. We stayed there the rest of that day to give our horses a little rest. The two Indians said they would go no farther, for I could find the way from there very well. As I left them, I said, "You may look for me back in a few days." "Don't try to come back this fall," they said, "for it is getting too late to cross the mountains, and we are apt to have a big snow storm at any time now. It will take you six days to get home from here, and that will make it too late for you to return. You stay at your home this winter and there will be Indians there next summer and you can come back with them."

They helped me pack my horses the next morning, put me on the right trail, and told me not to ride too fast, for I could get to the white settlement long before night. About noon, I came to some warm springs, and I thought it would be a good idea to wash my face and hands, as I had not done it very often during the last two years. I saw that I would have plenty of time for the sun was high, so I unpacked my horses and staked them nearby, undressed and went to work to give myself a good scrubbing. I ran my fingers through my hair and tried to get the snarls out, but after I was dressed again, I could not see that I looked any better. My hands were like an Indian's and my costume was in the latest Indian fashion. My leggings were made of new red flannel, my shirt of antelope skins, and my frock was heavy buckskin, smoked to a nice red color, and with beads of all colors in wide stripes down the breast and on the shoulders, and fringes all around the bottom that reached nearly to my knees. My cap was made of rawhide, with notches all around the top, and looked like a cross-cut saw turned upside down. It came to a peak in front, and mother put a crown in it with a musk-rat skin.

After I had scrubbed off all the dirt I could, I packed up and started again. I could see the little town long before I came to it, and at the first house I came to, a man had just driven up with a load of hay. I asked him if he could tell me where I could find a place to camp. He said I could stop there if I wanted to; that he had plenty of hay, and I was perfectly welcome, so I thought I would take him at his word. I unpacked my horses and tied them under a shed and gave them some hay. By that time, the man came out and said supper was ready. I told him I had plenty to eat with me and would rather not go in. "Come and eat with me," he said, and he took me by the hand and led me into the house. The women and children stared at me so that I did not know what to do. The children would look at me, then they would turn to one another and laugh. The lady said, "I guess you would like to wash before you eat," and she gave me some water and soap. It was the first soap I had seen for two years. After I had washed, she told me to sit down at the table; then the man asked me, "Don't you take your hat off when you eat?" I said, "No." He said, "Will you please take it off here?" I pulled it off. They had bread and butter and potatoes and gravy and milk—the first I had seen since I left home. You bet, I was glad when I got away from the table.

I went out and watered my horses and gave them some hay. By this time it was dark, so I made my bed and turned in. Just as I was getting into bed, I saw this man go down town and pretty soon he came back with three more men. I saw them go into the house and soon he came out to where I was and said the bishop was in the house and would like to have a talk with me. I said I did not want to talk, but he kept at me until I got up and went in.

The bishop said his name was Nichols, or something like that. He said, "I see by your dress that you have been with the Indians, have you not?" I told him that I had been with the Indians for a year or two. He said he had read in the papers a year or so ago about a little boy running off with the Indians, "And I should judge," said he, "that perhaps you are the boy." I said, "Maybe I am." He asked me what tribe I belonged to. I told him that I belonged to Washakie's tribe. He said, "I have heard that Washakie is a chief among the Shoshones, and that his tribe is friendly to the white people. But you can tell us more about them than anybody else can." I said that Washakie's Indians were good Indians, and that I heard Washakie say many times that he was a friend to the white people who lived in Utah, and that he had seen the big chief who was a very good tibo. "What is that?" he asked me. I said, "I forgot I was talking to a white man; 'tibo' means white man."

I told him he had no need to fear Washakie's tribe, but that old Pocatello had drawn away some of Washakie's Indians, that they were bad Indians, and were doing everything against the white people they could. I said they would steal cattle and horses, and would kill white people if they were found away from the settlements. Washakie says they are bad, and that they kill a great many emigrants and steal their horses and burn their wagons.

Well, this bishop talked and talked and asked me ten thousand questions. After a while the woman said, "Do let the poor boy rest." I told them I had always been in bed by dark and that I felt pretty tired. "Well," he said, "you can go to bed now, and I will see you in the morning. You had better come down to my house and stay all day. I would like very much for Brother Snow to have a talk with you." I thought that neither Snow nor rain would catch me in that place another day, so I was up by the peep of day, and away I went.

I traveled seven or eight miles and stopped at some more hot springs, unpacked my horses, and got me something to eat. I thought I would not stop any more in towns where bishops could get hold of me and talk my lungs out. I thought I would camp out by the side of the road after that.

Well, after my horses got filled up—I was already filled up from that bishop the night before—I started on my way again and traveled eight or ten miles and came to a place they called Ogden. As I was going down the main street a man standing by a store stopped me and began talking Indian to me. He asked where I had been. I told him. While we were talking a lot more men came up to us and one of them asked me where I was going to stop that night. I said I did not know, but that I would go down the road a piece until I found grass and water and then I would camp. He asked me to put my horses in a corral there and give them all they could eat. "No," said I, "I would rather go on." "No, you must stop here tonight," and he took the rope out of my hand and led my horses into the corral. I followed him, and when I unpacked, I asked if he was the bishop. He said he was. I told him I thought he was. He asked me why I thought he was the bishop. I said, "Because you talk so much." He laughed and said I must not notice anything like that for they seldom saw a person like me, and they wanted to find out all they could about the Indians. After a while he said, "Come into the house and we will have supper." I did not want to go, but he would have it that way, so I went in with him. I think he said his name was West.

This Bishop West, if that was his name, asked me quite a few questions, but he said he would not weary me by talking too long. I went to bed soon after dark that night, and I thought I would get off early the next morning and give them the slip again; but just as I was packing up, the bishop came out and said, "Hold on, there, you are not going before breakfast?" I told him I had plenty to eat along with me. "Well," he continued, "you will surely eat with me this morning." So I had to stop until after breakfast. He asked me a great many more questions, but he was very nice about it. I felt glad to talk with him, he was so kind and good to me.

He said I would be a very useful man if I was treated right. He asked me if I had been to school much, and was much surprised when I told him that I had never gone to school one day in my life. He said I must go to school, and if I lived near him he would see that I did go. When I started he asked me to go and see Brother Young when I got to Salt

Lake City. I thought I did not want any Brother Young in mine, but I was a young boy then, and did not know what I was talking about.

That day I got to a place they called Farmington. Just as I was nearing the town, I saw some boys driving cows. I asked them where I could camp. "Up on that mountain if you want to," said one. I said to him, "You think you are pretty smart, don't you?" He said, "I am smart enough for you, Mr. Injun. If you don't believe it, just get off that buzzard head and I will show you." I jumped off my horse and he ran. I got on again and started after them, but they got through a fence and ran away across the fields. I went on through the town and camped in a field, after getting permission from a man who lived near by, and I was not bothered with questions that night.

The next morning I was off pretty early and reached Salt Lake City, went through the city, and stopped at the Jordan bridge for noon. I knew where I was then, for I had been in the city a few times before. That afternoon I went on to what we called Black Rock, those days, and camped that night near the great Salt Lake. I was now within a short day's ride of home. Oh, home! sweet, sweet home! I could hardly stay there 'till morning, I wanted to get home so badly.

Just as I was making camp, a team drove up with three people in the wagon. I knew them. They were John Zundel, his sister Julia, and Jane Branden, my nearest neighbors when I was at home, but they did not know me at first. I had a fire, and was broiling a rabbit I had killed, when Julia came up to where I was and tried to get a good look at me, but I kept my face turned from her as much as I could. Finally she got a glimpse of my face and went to the wagon and I heard her say to Jane, "That is the whitest Indian I ever saw, and he has blue eyes." Jane said, "I'll bet a dollar it's Nick Wilson." Then they came to where I was and Jane said, "Look up here, young man, and let us see you." I looked at her. "I knew it was you, you little scamp!" and she took hold of me, shook me, patted me on my back, and said she had a notion to flog me. She said, "Your poor mother has nearly worried herself to death about you." I cannot begin to tell all that was said that night, but they told me that the soldiers were coming to kill the Mormons, and all of the men that had horses were out to stop them. They said that the whole country was in an uproar.

Well, morning came at last, and I packed up in a hurry and started for home, and I did not stop until I got there. I was mighty glad to see my dear old home again. As I rode up, two of my little sisters, who were playing by the side of the house, ran in and told mother that an Indian was out there. She came to the door and knew me as soon as she saw me. And, oh! my dear friends, I cannot tell you just what passed during the next hour, but they were all glad to have me back safe at home again. I forgot all about my horses, and when, finally, I thought of them and went out to unpack them, all the folks followed me and mother said, "Where did you get all those horses? Did you take them from the Indians and run away?" I told her they were mine, and that I had not run away from the Indians as I had done from her.

After I had put my horses in the field, I told them all about what I had seen and passed through while I was away, and answered everybody's questions the best I could.

CHAPTER XIV.

YEAR OF THE MOVE.

Soon after reaching home, another call was made for men to go out and stop the soldiers at Echo canyon. I wanted to go, but my father would not let me. I said I could kill soldiers with my bow and arrows as well as the others could with their old flint-lock guns, but they said I was too young, so my older brother went, and I let him have one of my buffalo robes and my roan pony.

All of the grain was not out of the field yet, and all of the men had gone off to the Echo Canyon war, except a few very old men who could not do much work. You could see the women and little boys out in the fields with oxen hauling grain and stacking it. There would be about half a dozen women to a team, with a little boy driving the oxen. I have seen as many as fifteen or twenty teams at a time out in the big public field hauling grain, and just as many women and children as could get around the wagons. They seemed to be as happy as larks, and you might hear the children singing in every part of the field:

"Old squaw-killer Harney is on the way, doo da;
He swears the Mormons he will slay, doo da, doo da,
    day."
Another song we used to sing ran something like
this:
"I looked to the west, and I looked to the east,
    And I saw General Johnston coming
With four white mules and a pack of d—n fools,
    And he landed on the other side of Jordan, O!"

Well, after the grain was all hauled, it had to
be threshed. An old man by the name of Baker, who
could just get around by the aid of two walking
sticks, took charge of the threshing machine. It was
not much like the steam threshers we have these
days. This one had a cylinder fixed in a big box,
and it was made to turn by what we called horse
power, but we had to turn it with ox power. Old
Daddy Baker, and as many women as could get
around the machine, started in to do the threshing.
We put on four yoke of oxen to run this old chaff
piler, as we called it.

Brother Baker put us oldest boys to pitch the
grain and feed it into the old machine. One of the
biggest boys started up the cattle and away she
went. I was to do the feeding. At first, the boys
pitched the grain so fast that I would let three or

four bundles in at a time and choke the old thing up and cause the belt to break, then it would take half an hour to get started again.

The straw and chaff and grain all came out together. About fifteen women with rakes would string out and rake the straw along until they left the grain behind, then about forty kids would stack the straw. After we threshed an hour or two we would stop and cave up, as we called it; that was pushing the grain and chaff into a pile to one side, then we would go on again. We would keep this up until we got through with Brother Martendial's job, then we would move the old rattle-trap over to Brother Pumpswoggle's place.

We had an old home-made fanning mill that would follow up the threshing machine and clean the chaff from the grain. Some of the women would take turns turning the old thing, while others would take milk pans and buckets and put the grain into the hopper, then the chaff would go one way and the grain the other. We would thresh only a hundred and fifty bushels a day, and we had over twenty thousand bushels to thresh, so you can see that it looked very discouraging, with winter so near.

As luck would have it, some of our men came in with a large band of mules and horses they had taken from the soldiers, and four of the men stopped at home to help with the threshing. 'Lonzo Mecham took charge of the threshing from that time on. We used some of our Uncle Sam's mules to do the rest of the threshing and got along first rate. They were good mules.

During the fall you could see the women hauling wood from the mountains, digging potatoes in the fields, and gathering in their garden and farm prodducts. Women that were hardly able to be out had to work like this while their husbands and fathers and brothers were away in the mountains defending their homes and families. They were poorly dressed, too, for cold weather.

Most of the people were very poor. The Indians and grasshoppers and crickets had kept them down so that it was hard for them to make a living at the best, and now there was a United States army coming to make a finish of us, and to hang every man, it was said, that had two wives, for they had ropes quite handy, and I believe they would have done it, too, if Lot Smith had not burned their wagon trains on the Sandy. After the Mormons got away with all the army's mules and cattle, and the snow became very deep in the mountains, the soldiers made winter camp on Ham's Fork, and most of our men came home, so we got our threshing done by the middle of the winter.

As poor as the people were, they were as happy as could be. We would have dances two or three times a week, and to pay the fiddler, we would take a peck of wheat or a peck of potatoes or carrots, or sometimes, a squash. My folks had raised some very fine squash that summer, and when I went to a dance, I would take a very large squash and get a few carrots back as change, and at recess my partner and I would eat the carrots for lunch. It may seem funny now to think of doing these things, but many people are yet living who remember them well, and they know we had very pleasant, happy times, too.

I said that the people were very poor. They were poor in house furniture, bedding, clothing, and such things, but we had plenty to eat and most of the people had cattle, sheep, hogs, and chickens. The people had been driven out of Missouri and Illinois and had traveled over thousands of miles to the Rocky Mountains to find a home where they could live in peace. In this long, rough journey, they had worn out their clothes and broken so much of their furniture and dishes that they had hardly any of these things left. Sometimes a coat or a dress would

be patched so many times and with so many different kinds of cloth that you could hardly tell which
kind of cloth it had been made of in the first place.

The people came that long, dreary journey
across the plains to find a place where they could
dwell in peace, but it seems that they were not to
be allowed to do this, for they were followed by bad
men who did all they could to cause these innocent
people more trouble. They wrote many lies about
the Mormons to the President of the United States,
until the government thought it had to do something, so it sent out a governor and a set of officers
with an army to investigate matters. After this
army had been driven into winter quarters in the
mountains, Brigham Young sent out and asked the
governor to come and find out for himself how
things were.

When spring came, things had not been fixed
up to suit all the officers, so the people of Utah
were ordered to leave their homes and move south.
Everybody had their crops in when the order came
to move. A guard was to remain to look after what
was left behind, and if it came to the worst, to burn
everything that might be useful to the army that
was expected. My father and his family and most
of our neighbors moved down to Spanish Fork, Utah,

where we stopped for further orders. I wanted to go back to live with Washakie and my dear, old, Indian mother, but I hated to leave until I found out what the army was going to do. By this time, I had traded my Crow pony for a white man's saddle and a two-year-old heifer.

While this move was going on, you could sit by the road-side for half a day and see any kind of outfit you might desire, from a wheel-barrow up to a fine, eight-mule team. An old wagon, with a cow and a horse hitched up together, was a common sight. You could see the finest buggies, drawn by big teams, or you could see one old ox hitched between the shafts of a rickety, old, two-wheeled cart. You could see women leading the family cow with their bedding and a little food packed on her back. So, some of these people were rich and many were poor, but they were all traveling the same road, and all appeared to be happy and none of them very badly scared.

We had not been in Spanish Fork long, when one day some Spaniards brought in a lot of wild horses to trade for cattle, and a good many folks had gathered around the corral to see the mustangs. While sitting on the corral fence, I saw a little black, three-year-old mare that took my fancy. I asked the man what he would take for her. He said, "I will sell her for sixty dollars, but if you will jump from that fence onto her back and ride her, you can have her for nothing." I said, "That is a whack, I'll do it." He told me to wait until they were ready to turn the horses out. It was not long before he said, "Now we are ready to see the fun." He had no idea whom he was talking to. He thought the colt would throw me off the first jump, and they would all have a good laugh on my account.

They let down the bars and drove the horses around so that the black colt came near enough for me to jump off the fence to her back. As she came around, I gave a jump and landed fairly on her back, and away she went out through the bars and down the street. It seemed as if every dog in town was after us. We passed through the town in no time, crossed the bridge, went up over the hill, and away off towards Pond Town. Then we circled around towards Goshen. We soon left behind the band of horses we started with, and ran away from all the dogs.

A man went over and told my folks that I was on a wild horse, that the horse was running away with me, and that I would be killed. Mother was not much worried, for she knew I had been on a wild

horse before. My brother mounted my pinto pony
as soon as he could and followed me, but when he
got to me, the colt I was riding had run itself down
and had stopped. He rode up and handed me a rope
which I put around the colt's neck, and then got off
to let her rest. After a while I mounted her again
and my brother drove her back to town.

When we got back, all of the men that had seen
us start off came up to see the colt. Among them
was one, Mr. Faust, Doc. Faust, they called him. He
said I beat all the boys riding he ever saw; that he
had a great many horses he wanted broke, and if I
would go with him he would give me fifty dollars a
month. When I told mother about it she said I
could not go, for my father was very sick, and she
was afraid he was not going to live much longer.

We stayed in the neighborhood of Spanish Fork
until about the first of August, when word came
that we could go back home, that everything was
fixed up with the officers all right, and that the
soldiers were going to pass through Salt Lake City
and on to Cedar Valley, where they intended
to build a fort.

We all started for home with a "hurrah!" and
when we got back, we all went to work with a will,
and I never saw such crops as we raised that year.

We raised from fifty to seventy-five bushels of wheat to the acre. All through Utah it was the same. That fall, wheat sold for five dollars and eight dollars a bushel, and the best of it was, everybody had plenty of it to sell. Wheat straw that winter sold at from forty to sixty dollars a ton, and hay brought from seventy-five to one hundred dollars a ton.

The harvesting all had to be done by hand, for there were no reaping machines in those days. We hired Owen Baston to cradle our grain, and my brother and I bound it. That fall, after we got the wheat all cut, my father died.

After the death of my father, my brother and I could not get along very well together. He was a very hard worker, and I had never done much work, and it went pretty hard with me. I would rather ride horses than work, so I thought I would go over to Mr. Faust and help him break horses for a while, and then I would go back to Washakie.

Mr. Faust lived in the south end of Rush Valley, Utah. When I got to his ranch, Mr. Faust was very glad to see me. He said to his other riders: 'We will have that old outlaw of a horse broken now, for here is a boy that will ride him as long as he has hair in his tail." I told him that I did not know about that, for I had not ridden a bad horse for more than a year. He said, "What do you call that jumping off the fence onto a wild mustang?" I said that she was not a bad animal to ride, for she did nothing but run. He said his horses were not bad to break, only this one had thrown two or three of the boys and that made him mean; "but," he said, "I want him broke, for he is about as good a horse as I have, and I know you can break him."

The next morning one of Mr. Faust's best riders and I went out to bring in the band that the outlaw was with. This man told me if I was not a very good rider that I had better keep off of that horse or he would kill me. I said I was not a very good rider, but I was not afraid to try him anyhow. So we brought in the band and roped the outlaw. Mr. Faust came out and said, "Well, what do you think about old Outlaw? Do you think you can ride him?" I said I would try. Mr. Faust said, "That's the stuff! I bet you can ride him." Then the man that had been talking to me and telling me to stay off the horse, told Mr. Faust not to let me ride him for he was sure to kill me.

I began to think that this man did not want me to ride the horse because he had been thrown by him two or three times. He was afraid I might prove to be the better rider. So I piled on Mister Outlaw and he started off all right. I rode him around a little and began to think they were making a fool of me, when pretty soon the old boy turned loose and fairly made my neck pop. He did the hardest bucking I ever saw, but he did it straight ahead. He didn't whirl like some horses do, so I stayed with him all right. When he stopped bucking, I sent him through for ten miles about as fast as he ever went, and when I got back to the ranch, I rode up to the corral where the man was saddling another horse, and, standing up in my saddle, I said, "Do you call this a bad horse? If you do, you don't know what a bad horse is." That man didn't like me very much after that. I got along with old Outlaw first rate after that, but I had to give him some very hard rides before he finally gave up and acknowledged me the master.

CHAPTER XV.

THE PONY EXPRESS.

About the time I was thinking of starting to re-join my Indian friends, the word came that the pony express was going to start, and Mr. Faust induced me to stay and be one of the pony riders. I sold my roan pony to a sergeant in Camp Floyd for seventy-five dollars, and I sold the little black mare for one hundred dollars. I took part of the money to mother and bought some clothes with the rest.

A great pow wow was going on about the pony express coming through the country. They had started to build roads and stations. These stations had to be built every ten miles apart and as near to water as possible. Well, the time came for the express horses to be strung along the line, and the riders were sent to their stations. Mr. Faust and Mr. Howard Egan went my bonds, and I was sent out west into Nevada to a station called Ruby Valley. This station was a home station and was kept by a man named William Smith, and Smith had a hostler whose name was Samuel Lee.

When we were hired to ride the express we had to go before a Justice of the Peace and swear that we would at all times be at our post, and not at any time be over one hundred yards from the station, except when we were carrying the mail. When we started out we were never to turn back, no matter what happened, until the mail was delivered at the next home station. We had to be ready to start back at a half-minute's notice, let it be day or night, rain or shine, Indians or no Indians.

Our saddles, which were all furnished by the company, had nothing to them but the bare tree, stirrups, and cinch. Two large pieces of sole leather about sixteen inches wide by twenty-four inches long were laced together with a strong leather string and thrown over the saddle. Fastened to these were four pockets, two in front and two behind on either side of the saddle. The two hind ones were the largest. The one in front on the left side was called the "way pocket." All of these pockets were locked with small padlocks and each home station keeper had a key to the way pocket. When the express arrived at the home station, the keeper would unlock the way pocket, and if there were any letters for the boys between the home stations, the rider would distribute them as he went along, and there was, also, a card in the way pocket that the station keeper would take out and put down on it the time the express got to this station and when it went out. He would tell the rider what time he would have to make up on his run if the express was behind time.

Well, the time came that we had to start. The express would leave St. Joseph, Missouri, and Sacramento, California, at the same time every day. The home stations were from forty to sixty miles apart, and one man's ride was from one home station to another. Between the home stations were other stations, ten miles apart, where horses could be changed. Not many riders could stand the long, fast riding at first, but after they had ridden for about two weeks they would be all right. At first the rider would be charged up with the saddle he was riding, and the first wages were kept back for it, and if we had no revolver and had to get one from the company, that would be forty dollars more to come out of our wages. Many a poor boy was killed by the Indians before he got the company paid for these things. Our wages were too small for the hard work we did, and the dangers we went through.

Everything went along first rate for a while, but after six or eight months of that kind of work the big, fine horses began to play out, then the com-

The Scout

pany sent to California and bought up all of the wild horses they could get, brought them in. strung them along the road, and put the best riders to breaking them. Peter Neece, our home station keeper, was a big, strong man, and a good rider. He was put to breaking some of these wild mustangs for the boys on his beat. After these wild horses had been ridden two or three times, they would be put on the regular line for the express boys to ride. Generally just as soon as the hostler could lead them in and out of the stable without getting his head kicked off, they were considered broke, and very likely they had just been handled enough to make them mean. I found it to be so with most of the horses they gave me to ride.

I was not a bit afraid of the Indians, but for some reason or other, the way they had told these big yarns about the Indians killing the riders rather worked me up, so that while I could not say I was afraid of them, I was pretty badly scared, just the same.

Well, my home station was at Shell Creek. I rode from Shell Creek to Deep Creek, and one day the Indians killed the rider out on the desert, and when I was to meet him at Deep Creek, why, he was not there. I had to keep right on until I met him. I went to the next station, Willow Creek, the first station over the mountain, and there I found out that he had been killed. My horse was about jaded by this time, so I had to stay here to let him rest. I would have had to start back in the night as soon as the horse got so he could travel, if those Indians had not come upon us.

About four o'clock in the afternoon, seven Indians rode up to the station and asked for something to eat. Peter Neece, the station keeper, picked up a sack with about twenty pounds of flour in it and offered it to them, but they would not have that little bit, they wanted a sack of flour apiece. Then he threw it back into the house and told them to get out, and that he wouldn't give them a thing.

This made them pretty mad, and as they passed a shed about four or five rods from the house, they each shot an arrow into a poor, old, lame cow, that happened to be standing there under the shed. When Neece saw them do that, it made him mad, too, and he jerked out a couple of pistols and commenced shooting at them. He killed two of the Indians and they fell off their horses right there. The others ran. He said, ''Now, boys, we will have a time of it, tonight. There are about thirty of those Indians camped up in the canyon there, and they will be upon us as soon as it gets dark, and we shall have to fight.''

A man by the name of Lynch happened to be there at the time. He had bragged a good deal about what he would do and we looked upon him as a sort of desperado and a very brave man. I felt pretty safe until he weakened and commenced to cry, then I wanted all of us to get on our horses and skip for the next station; but Pete said, ''No. We will load up all the old guns that are around here and be ready for them when they come. There are four of us, and we can stand off the whole bunch of them.'' Well, just a little before dark, we could see a big dust over towards the mouth of the canyon, and we knew they were coming. It was about six miles from the canyon to the station.

Pete thought it would be a good thing to go out a hundred yards or so, and lie down in the brush and surprise them as they came up. When we got out there he had us lie down about four or five feet apart. ''Now,'' he said, ''when you fire, jump out to one side, so if they shoot at the blaze of your gun, you will not be there.'' We all took our places, and, you bet, I lay close to the ground. Pretty soon we could hear their horses' feet striking the ground, and it seemed to me as if there were thousands of them; and such yells as they let out, I never heard before. The sounds were coming straight towards us, and I thought they were going to run right over us.

It was sandy where we lay, with little humps here and there, and scrubby grease-wood were growing on the humps. Finally the Indians got close enough for us to shoot. Pete shot and jumped away to one side. I had two pistols, one in each hand, cocked all ready to pull the trigger, and was crawling on my elbows and knees. Each time he would shoot, I saw him jump. Soon they were all shooting, and each time they shot, I would jump. I never shot at all.

After I had jumped a good many times, I happened to land in a little wash, or ravine, that the water had made. I guess my back came pretty nearly level with the top of it. Anyway, I pressed myself down so I could get right in. I don't know how I felt, I was so scared. I lay there and listened until I could hear no more shooting, but I thought I could hear the horses' hoofs beating on the hard ground near me, until I found out it was only my heart beating. After a while, I raised my head a little and looked off towards the desert, and I could see those humps of sand covered with grease-wood.

They looked exactly like Indians on horses, and I could see several of them near the wash.

I crouched down again and lay there for a long time, maybe two hours. Finally everything was very still, so I thought I would go around and see if my horse was where I had staked him, and if he was, I would go back to my station over in Deep Creep and tell them that the boys were all killed and I was the only one that had got away all right. Well, as I went crawling around the house on my elbows and knees, just as easy as I could, with both pistols ready, I saw a light shining between the logs in the back part of the house. I thought the house must be full of the Indians, so I decided to lie there awhile and see what they were doing, anyhow. I lay there for some time, listening and watching, and then I heard one of the men speak right out a little distance from the house, and say, "Did you find anything of him?" Another man answered, "No, I guess he is gone." Then I knew it was the boys, but I lay there until I heard the door shut, then I slipped up and peeped through the crack and saw that all three of them were there all right. I was most too much ashamed to go in, but finally I went around and opened the door. When I stepped in Pete called out, "Hello! Here he is. How far did you chase them? I knew you would stay with them. I told the fellows here that you would bring back at least half a dozen of them." I think they killed five Indians that night. The next morning I went back to Deep Creek.

I was sent further west, about three hundred miles, to ride from the Carson Sink to Fort Churchill. The distance was about seventy-five miles and was a very hard ride for the horses as well as for me, because much of the distance was through deep sand. Some things were not so bad, however, for I had no mountains to cross, the winter was mild, and the Indians were a little more friendly here. East of my beat, along Egan Canyon, Shell Creek, and Deep Creek, the Indians had begun to be very saucy, and they had threatened to burn the stations and kill the people, and in the following spring they did break out in good earnest, burned some of the stations and killed one of the riders. That same spring I was changed back into Major Egan's divison, and rode from Shell Creek to Ruby Valley.

That summer the Indians got very bad. They burned several stations, killed the hostlers, and also a few riders. I got very badly wounded that summer. I had been taking some horses to Antelope station, and on my way back I made a stop at

Spring Valley station. When I got there the two
boys that looked after the horses at the station were
out on the woodpile playing cards, and they wanted
me to stay with them and have dinner. I got off my
horse and started him towards the stable, but instead of going to the stable he went behind it, where
some other horses were grazing.

Pretty soon we saw the horses going across the
meadow towards the cedars with two Indians on
foot behind them. We started after them full tilt,
and gained on them a little, and as we ran I fired
three shots at them from my revolver, but they were
too far off for me to hit them. They reached the
cedars a little before we did. I was ahead of the
other two boys, and as I ran around a large cedar,
one of the Indians, who had hidden behind a tree,
shot me in the head with a flint spiked arrow. The
arrow struck my head about two inches above the
left eye. The other two boys were on the other
side of the tree, and seeing the Indian run, came
around to find out where I was and found me lying
on the ground with the arrow sticking in my head.

They tried to pull the arrow out, but the shaft
came away and left the flint spike in my head.
Thinking that I would surely die, they rolled me
under a tree and started for the next station as fast

as they could go. There they got a few men and came back the next morning to bury me, but when they got to me and found I was still alive they thought they would not bury me just then. They decided to wait awhile. They carried me to a station that was called Cedar Wells, and from there sent to Ruby station for a doctor. When he came, he took the spike out of my head and told the boys to keep a wet rag on the wound and that was all they could do for me. I lay there for six days, when Major Egan happened to come along, and seeing that I was still alive, sent for the doctor again, and when the doctor came and saw that I was no worse he started to do something for me. I lay for eighteen days and did not know anything, then I began to get better fast, and it was but a little while until I was riding again. I think if Mr. Egan had not come along when he did I would not be here now telling about it. But, Oh! how I have suffered with my head at times since then.

The Indians kept getting worse. They had attacked emigrant trains, and had done a lot of damage to the express line by burning stations, killing the riders, and running off with the horses. The Indians got so bad that it was hard to keep riders enough to carry the express, for every one that could leave would do so, and it was hard for the agents to hire men to take their places. The company had to raise the wages from forty dollars a month to sixty, and it was hard to get men even at that price.

Between Deep Creek and Shell Creek was a station we called Eight-Mile station, kept by an old man, and he had two young emigrant boys to help him.

Their mother had died east of Salt Lake City with the cholera, and when they got out here, their father was shot by the Indians, and he died when they reached Deep Creek, and left these two boys with the station keeper. The father gave him five hundred dollars in money, a big pair of mules, and a new wagon, if he would send the boys back to their relatives in Missouri, where the family came from.

It was too late to send them back that fall, so the boys had to pass the winter there with him. The old man that kept Eight-Mile station couldn't do the work very well, so the older of the two boys was allowed to go there and help him. Well, along came an emigrant train, and the old man slipped away with the emigrants and left the boy to take care of the station alone.

It was hard to get men to come out here when the Indian troubles began, and the boy wanted to keep the station and have his brother come up from Deep Creek and help him.

One day, while the two boys were tending the station, I rode up there to meet the other rider, and as I reached the station I could see him coming five or six miles out. While we were watching him, a lot of Indians broke out of the brush and took in after him. He made a great race for it, but just before he reached the station they shot and killed him. We knew the Indians would attack the station, so we hurried to the barn and brought three horses to the house.

The station house was a rock building, twelve by twenty feet, with a shed roof covered with earth so that no timbers were sticking out that the Indians could set fire to. There were portholes in each end of the building, and one on each side of the door in front.

We succeeded in getting the three horses into this house by the time the Indians surrounded the station. They kept shooting at the back of the house, for they soon learned not to come up in front of those portholes.

We killed one or two of them that were foolish

them, an Indian's horse fell, carrying his rider down with him, and as Kennedy charged on the Indian to run over him he received an arrow in the arm, but the Indian got a bullet through his head in return. Kennedy had to wait until we came up to pull the arrow out of his arm.

By that time the Indians had the horses in a box canyon, where the rocks were very steep on both sides. A few Indians hid among the rocks and held us back while the rest of the band rushed the horses on up the canyon. The entrance to the conyon led south for a few hundred yards, and then turned sharply around a large, steep mountain, and ran almost directly north. A short distance after it turned, the canyon opened out into a large meadow about a mile long.

When we saw that we could not pass the Indians to get to the horses, Kennedy thought it would be best to go back two or three miles and cross a low divide, and so get into the canyon at the head of the meadows. The canyon narrowed again here and he thought we might head the Indians off if we could get there first.

So we turned and went back about two miles and a half to go over this divide. When we got near the top of the divide there was a cliff of rock too steep to get the horses over, so we tied them in a clump of mountain mahogany growing nearby, and went on afoot. We could not go down the other side very fast, for the white maple brush was very thick, with a pine tree now and then.

Just before we got down to the head of the meadows, we stopped on the side of the mountain near a very large, flat-topped rock. Kennedy sat up on the rock, watching for the Indians to come out onto the meadows from the canyon below. The rest of us went down just below the rock and filled our pockets with "yarb," or Indian tobacco, that grew there. While picking the yarb, Frank Mathis laid his old, muzzle-loading, Springfield rifle down in the bushes, where he could reach it when he wanted it.

We were there about half an hour, when all at once Kennedy jumped down among us and cried, "My God! boys, we're surrounded!" In the excitement that followed, Mathis grabbed his gun by the muzzle and gave it a jerk. The hammer caught on a bush and the gun was discharged, and shot his left arm off between the shoulder and the elbow. That rattled us quite a bit, so we hardly knew what to do next.

Kennedy thought it was best for us to fight our

way back to where our horses were tied. So he
started Mathis up the hill ahead of the rest of us.
We were to keep the Indians back if we could. We
knew they were around us on every side, for we
could hear the brush crack and see it shake every
once in a while. When near the top we came to a
bare stretch of ground about two rods across.

We stopped in the edge of the brush, for we
knew the Indians could shoot us very easily as soon
as we got in the open. Kennedy thought we had
better make a break for it and scatter out as we
ran, so the Indians could not hit us so easily. I
was the shortest legged one in the lot, but I wasn't
the last one over, just the same. When we were
about half way across, the Indians began to shoot
at us with their arrows and guns. A bullet struck
a rock right beneath my feet, and it helped me over
the hill just that much the quicker.

By the time we got down to our horses, Mathis
was bleeding badly. He was faint and begging for
water. We had to lead our horses down to the bottom of the mountain on account of the rocks. Kennedy sent me and Robert Orr down to the creek to
bring water back in our hats for Mathis. When
we got back with the water, Kennedy sent me on

to the station, so I could be there when the express
came and be ready to take it on.

That is the last time I ever saw Frank Mathïs.
He was a brave man and a good Indian fighter. He
was taken to Salt Lake, so he could be better cared
for. After he got well, he and a man by the name
of Eccles stole eight government mules from Camp
Douglas and started with them for Montana. They
were followed by the soldiers, and both of them
were overhauled and killed in the Malad Valley.
That was the last of poor Frank Mathis.

About the time the Indians were at their worst,
a small train of emigrants came through on their
way to California. They were told by all of the
station agents that it was not safe for so few people
to travel through the country at that time, and that
they had better stop until more trains came up.
They said they were well armed, and thought they
could stand off the Indians all right. At that time
I was riding from Shell Creek through Egan Canyon
to Ruby Valley. We all knew that this train would
be attacked somewhere between Deep Creek and
Ruby Valley.

We, who were acquainted with the Gosiute Indians, could tell when they were going to make a
raid, for they would make signs on the mountains

with smokes by day and fires by night, and so by these signs we knew that this train would be attacked as they were going through some of the bad canyons on the route. Egan Canyon was about the worst of these. It was a narrow canyon about six miles long, with cliffs on each side from three hundred to one thousand feet high, so that you could turn neither to the right nor to the left. This canyon was a dread to all that had to go through it.

The train of emigrants entered this canyon just ahead of me. I rode very fast that day to try to overtake them before they got to the worst part of it, but just before I reached them I could hear shooting, then I knew that the Indians were onto them. I stopped a moment to listen, when I saw two men coming. They were bare-headed and were running for dear life. When they got near, they said, "Go back. The whole company has been killed but us." They passed me and went on.

After a little while I could hear no more shooting, and I started and rode slowly up the canyon. At every turn around a point I would stop and listen and have a look. Soon the wagons came in sight and I stopped and looked a while, but I could not see anything of the Indians. Then I went up to the wagons, and such a terrible sight I never saw before. Dead men, women, and children were strewn all around the wagons. The tugs of the harness had been cut and the mules and horses were gone. I rode to the next point, and as no Indians were in sight I knew they had gone, so I went back to the wagons to see if any little children might have been overlooked by the Indians.

One woman I found lying by the side of the road who was not quite dead. She was lying on her side with her face up and her black hair spread out over a small sage brush. She gave one gasp as I rode up. I spoke to her, but she made not another move. She was dead. I cannot describe my feelings as I sat there on my horse, but I know the tears ran down my cheeks very fast as I gazed on this scene. I saw four little babes, all under one year old, lying by a wagon wheel where they had been killed, and I could see blood on the hub of the wheel where their little heads had been struck.

After I found that they were all dead, I could not stand it to look upon this dreadful scene any longer, so I started on my way. When I got out of the canyon and saw where the Indians had turned off the road, I did not spare my horse until I reached the station. The station keeper sent a messenger to Ruby Valley, where the soldiers were, and they came and buried the dead emigrants.

CHAPTER XVI.

JOHNSTON PUNISHES THE INDIANS.

The Indians became so troublesome that the soldiers from Camp Floyd were called out to stop their dreadful work. I got a letter from Major Egan directing me to meet him at Camp Floyd as soon as I could get there, for they wanted me for interpreter and guide for the soldiers. I started at once and made two hundred miles in three days. When I reached Camp Floyd, General Albert Sidney Johnston was all ready to start out against the Indians with four companies of soldiers. We traveled west, and crossed the Great American Desert in the night, so as not to be seen by the Indians.

The soldiers stayed at Fish Springs and sent me out with three other scouts to see if we could find any signs of the Indians we were after. We took only two days' rations with us. The first day we met with no success, so the next morning we separated. I sent two of the scouts to circle around to the south, and took with me a young man by the name of Johnson, and we went northwest. That afternoon we saw two Indians crossing a valley.

We kept out of sight but followed them until night, and saw them go into a small bunch of cedars. We left our horses and slipped up as close to them as we could without letting them see us.

When we got pretty near to them, I recognized in one of the Indians my old friend Yaiabi; but not feeling sure that he would be glad to see me, I told Johnson to have his shooting-irons ready and I would go up to them and see what they would do. As soon as they saw me coming they jumped up and drew their bows. I began to talk to them in their language. Yaiabi did not recognize me at first, and demanded to know what I was doing there. I told him I wanted water. He said there was no water except a very little they had brought with them. They asked me if I was alone. I told them that another young man was with me, then I called to Johnson to come up.

After Yaiabi found out who I was he felt better, for they were very uneasy at first. When I asked him how he came to be there, he said they had been out to a little lake to see some Parowan indians that were camped there. I asked him what the Indians were doing there. He said they were waiting for some more of the Pocatello Indians to come, and as soon as they arrived they were going

to burn all the stations and kill all of the riders and
station keepers. I asked him if he was going with
them. He said he was not. Then I asked him why
he had been over to see those Indians. He said
that the Parowan Indians had stolen his sister's little boy two years before, and he went out to see if
he could find the child. I asked if he had found
it. He said, "No. They have sold it to the white
folks." "Do you know when the Indians they are
looking for will be there?" He replied that they
would be there the next night.

I knew it was a big day's ride back to where
the Indians were gathering and I knew it was a
hard day's ride to the place where the soldiers were
camped. I did not know what was best for me to
do. I had these two Indians and I did not want to
let them go, for I was afraid they would skip back
and let the others know that the soldiers were after
them. Here we were a big day's ride to water, and
our horses had had none since early morning, so
I decided that it would be better to take the Indians
to headquarters and let General Johnston decide
what to do. I told Yaiabi my plans. He said he
did not want to go to the soldiers, for he was afraid
of them. I told him I would see that the soldiers
did him no harm. He said, "Yagaiki, you have

known me ever since you were a little boy, and you never knew of my doing anything bad in your life.'' I told him I knew that he had always been a good Indian, ''but now you know that the soldiers are after those bad Indians and intend to kill the last one of them, and if I let you go, you will go to them and tell them that the soldiers are after them. Then if General Johnston should find out what I had done he would think I stood in with the Indians and would have me shot, so, you see, you must go with us to the soldiers' camp.''

The Indian that was with Yaiabi said he would not go to the soldiers' camp, and started to get his bow, but I had my pistol on him in a jiffy and told him to stand. He stopped, and I kept him there while Johnson gathered up their bows and arrows. When I told them to get ready to start, Yaiabi said they were tired and would like to stay there until morning, but I said that our horses were so thirsty, we had better travel in the cool of the night or we would not be able to get them to camp, so we set out for Fish Springs.

I told Johnson to tie the bows and arrows to his saddle and to keep a close watch over them; Yaiabi mounted my horse while I walked and led the horse. When I got tired of walking, I changed

places with Yaiabi, and then young Johnson walked
and let the other Indian ride his horse. In this way
we traveled until morning. When daylight came, I
gave the bows and arrows to young Johnson and
told him to go to General Johnston's camp as soon
as possible and send us fresh horses and some water.
In about six hours he came back to us, accompanied
by two soldiers with some water and two extra
horses for the Indians to ride. By traveling pretty
fast, we reached camp at one o'clock that day.

General Johnston was very much pleased with
me for bringing the two Indians in. At the sight
of so many soldiers the Indians were very uneasy,
but after they had been given something to eat and
saw that they were not going to be hurt, they felt
much better.

General Johnston talked with the Indians for
about an hour, and I acted as interpreter. Yaiabi
told him just how the big camp of Indians was lo-
cated, and said there were about three hundred
warriors there then; they were looking for about
fifty more to join them that night, and as soon as
they could complete their plans they were going to
burn the stations and kill all the white men they
could find. He thought they would be ready in
about five days to begin their bloody work.

The general was very much pleased by the way
Yaiabi talked. He called him a good Indian, and
said he believed he was telling the truth. I told
Yaiabi what the general said. General Johnston
told me to get a little rest, for he wanted me to
start out again that night if I would. I lay down
and had a little sleep, and when I got up he told
me that I was to go to the lake and see if Yaiabi
had told the truth; and if everything was all right,
to send back word as soon as I could by one of the
scouts that he would send with me. He said for
me to do all my traveling at night and keep under
cover in the day time, and to meet him as soon as
I could at a spring about half way between where
we were and the Indians. Then on the following
night he would move his soldiers to another spring
which Yaiabi had told about, and which was within
six miles of the lake where the Indians were
gathering.

About dark, three of us started with four days'
rations. I rode the little pinto pony on this trip,
the first I had ridden him for a long time. We
traveled all night and reached the first spring just
at daybreak. I knew it would be a hard night's
ride to go from here to the lake and then reach
Yaiabi's spring in the mountains before daylight.

About midnight we arrived at the north end
of the lake, which was only a mile and a half long
and half a mile wide. I had my two scouts stop
there while I wrapped a red blanket around me and
went on foot to find out what I could about the
Indian camp. I had gone only a few steps when I
came to a lot of horses, and as I was passing around
them I heard an Indian speak to his horse. I went
he was hobbling his horse, that he had staked him
he was hobbling his horse, that he had staked him
but was afraid he might hurt himself in the rope,
and that he had ridden him pretty hard that day.
I asked him if he had come with the Pocatello Indians. He said he had, and that seventeen others
came with him. "We will start burning the stations, then, soon," I said. "Were you at the council tonight?" he asked. I told him I was not at
the council, that I had been following a horse that
had started back. He said that at the council it
was decided that the Parowans were to go to Ruby
Valley and burn and kill everything they came to;
and that the Pocatello Indians and the Gosiutes were
to start at Ibapah and burn towards the east.
I asked him when we were to start from
there. He said, "In four days." We were
walking towards their camp as we talked, so

as soon as I found out all I wanted to know I said that I had forgotten my rope and would have to go back for it. So I parted company with my Indian friend. He was a Shoshone, and he thought I was another. When I got out of his sight, I wasn't long getting back to where I had left the boys, and in a very short time one of them was carrying the news to the army.

The other scout and I went to find the spring Yaiabi had told me about. We got well into the mountains before daylight, and when it was light enough to see, we found the spring up a very rough canyon. We staked our horses so they could get plenty to eat and then crawled off into the willows for a good nap.

That afternoon I climbed a high mountain near-by to see which would be the best way to go from there to the Indians' camp in the night. After I had studied the lay of the country pretty well, I went back to the horses, ate a little cold lunch, and when it commenced to get dark, we struck out to meet General Johnston at the appointed place.

We did not travel very fast, for I knew we would reach the place before the soldiers could get there. We were at the spring about two hours be-fore day light, and had a good nap before General

Johnston came. When he got to us he wanted to know if I thought it safe to make a fire to boil some coffee. I told him I thought there was no danger, so we made a small fire and had a good cup of coffee, then we all lay down for a little sleep.

About sundown, the packers began loading the hundred pack mules we had with us, and we got started just about dark for the Yaiabi spring which was about six miles north of the Indians' camp. We reached the spring in good time, and were all unpacked before dawn.

After breakfast, General Johnston and I went up on to the mountain so that he could see the Indian camp. He had a good pair of field glasses and could see everything very plainly. He asked if I knew anything about that bunch of willows he could see a little to the west of their camp. I told him I knew it very well, for when the express first started it came this way, and we had a station right where the Indian camp is now, so I had been there many times. He said, "Then you can take me to it in the night?" I told him I could, and pointed out to him the way we would have to go. He told me he wanted to make the attack the next morning at daybreak. We went back to camp, and found all the soldiers asleep, except the guard; and in a very

short time we were rolled in our blankets and
dreaming of the time when all the Indians would be
good Indians.

When I awoke that afternoon, I saw General
Johnston and his staff going up the mountain to
where we had been that morning. They got back to
camp just before sundown, and held a hasty council with the remainder of the officers, then orders
were given to pack up, and we got in line just at
dark. I told General Johnston he would have to
take his men down this canyon in single file, and in
some places we would have to travel along the side
of the mountain over very narrow trails; that we
would have to climb above high cliffs, and pass
through some very dangerous places. He said for
me to go ahead, and when I came to the bad places
to dismount and they would follow suit. We had
about two miles to go before we would come to the
bad places, and when I got off the next man would
get off and so on down the line. By doing this, we
got down the canyon very well, except that three
of our pack mules rolled over a cliff and were killed.

The head of the company got out of the canyon
about eleven o'clock that night. We were within
six or seven hundred yards of the Indian camp, for
the lake lay almost at the foot of the mountains. As
the soldiers came down they formed into lines, and

General Johnston and I started to find the bunch of willows we had seen from the top of the mountain. We soon found it, and went back to the soldiers. The general said that was all he wanted with me until after the fight, and for me to take care of the two Indians we had with us. So I got Yaiabi and his friend, and we climbed a small hill not far away, where we could see the fight when it commenced.

The soldiers didn't all get out of the canyon until about three o'clock in the morning, and the pack train was not all out when daylight came. In the meantime, General Johnston had strung the soldiers around the Indian camp.

Just as day was breaking, an old Indian chief started a fire in front of his wickiup, and was standing there calling to some of the other Indians, when a soldier shot him without orders. Then the fight commenced. Oh, my! how the guns did rattle! It was almost too dark at first for me to see much of the fight, but it was getting lighter all the time. I asked Yaiabi if he was not afraid that his people would all be killed. He said he was a Mormon, and those Indians were all bad Indians, so he did not care very much which whipped—the Indians or the soldiers. As we were coming down the canyon that night, the General gave me his field glasses to carry for him and I still had them.

Along the edge of the lake grew a lot of bulrushes. Soon after the firing began, I could see the papooses running into these rushes and hiding. From the volleys that were fired it got so smoky that I could not see very plainly, but the shooting soon stopped, and as the smoke raised, I could see everything that was going on. By this time, they were in a terrible mixup, and were fighting fiercely, the soldiers with their bayonets and sabers, and the Indians with their clubs, axes, and knives. I could see little children not over five or six years old with sticks fighting like wild cats. I saw a soldier and an Indian that had clinched in a death struggle. They had each other by the hair of the head, and I saw a squaw run up to them with an ax and strike the soldier in the back and he sank to the ground, then she split his head with the ax. While she was doing this, a soldier ran a bayonet through her, and that is the way it was going over the whole battle ground. And, what a noise they made! with the kids squalling, the squaws yelling, the bucks yelping, the dogs barking, and the officers giving their orders to the soldiers.

This was the worst battle and the last one that I ever saw. It lasted about two hours, and during that short period of time, every Indian, squaw, and papoose, and every dog was killed. After the battle, I was sent to bring up the baggage wagons to haul our wounded to Camp Floyd. General Johnston made me a present of one hundred dollars, and I didn't know any better than to take it.

As we were on our way back to Camp Floyd with the wounded, and were passing through a rocky canyon, we were fired at by some straggling Indian, and I was shot through my left arm about half way between the wrist and the elbow. The same bullet that went through my arm killed a soldier at my side. The one shot was all we heard, and we did not even see the one who fired it. I have sometimes wondered if that bullet was not sent especially for me.

That spring the great war between the North and the South broke out, and General Johnston sold all of the government cattle and wagons very cheap, and went back East with his pack mules. I bought a yoke of oxen for eighteen dollars and a new wagon for ten. There must have been as many as ten thousand oxen bought at from twenty-five to fifty dollars a yoke. That summer the gold mines were opened in Montana and everything had to be hauled with ox teams, and the same oxen we had bought for eighteen dollars, were worth from one hundred and fifty to two hundred dollars a yoke. The poor people that had been living on greens and lumpy-dick for two or three years, now began to get very wealthy, and proud. The young ladies began to wear calico dresses, and I even saw young men who could afford to wear calico shirts and soldiers' blue overcoats and smoke store tobacco. A few even got so wealthy that they apostatized.

CHAPTER XVII.

THE OVERLAND STAGE.

Just before the soldiers left Camp Floyd, the Overland stage line was opened from St. Joseph, Missouri, to Sacramento, California. Shortly afterward the telegraph line was completed across the continent. This ended the work of the Pony Express. Instead of the pony riders dashing on their wiry horses over prairies and mountain and desert, now came the stage drivers with their sturdy horses, four or six-in-hand, rolling along in their great Concord Coaches, loaded with passengers, mail and express.

The stations, as before, were scattered along the trail from eight to sixteen miles apart, according to the water. These stations were mainly low dirt-roofed structures, built of logs or adobes or rock. After Johnston's army had decamped, the lumber left by them at Camp Floyd was used for some stations. They were large enough to accommodate six to eight horses, and had partitioned from the stalls one room for the stable keepers and another for provisions. Grain was hauled to them

from the fields of Utah and California. Native
hay was supplied from the grassy valleys through
which the route lay. Traveling blacksmiths kept
the horses shod, and the stages in repair.

As a few of the stations had to be built where
there was no spring or stream, it was necessary to
haul water to them. This was my first work in
connection with the Overland stage. I had a good
four horse team and was given the job of supplying
Canyon station with water.

One day while I was unloading the water the
stage came into this station. Major Howard Egan,
who had charge of this division of the route, had
the lines. The stage driver lay dead in "the boot"
and one passenger was wounded. They had been
shot by stage robbers, or "road agents," as we
called them. Another driver must be had. The
station keepers said they couldn't drive four horses,
so Major Egan called on me. I hadn't had any
experience handling the stage, but I tried it. The
Major seemed to think I drove all right, for he
didn't send any man to relieve me as he promised
to do, so I kept on driving. Finally I sold my
team and water outfit and became a regular stage-
driver. For about two years I kept on swinging
over the rough and heavy roads through the

deserts of Nevada in "the boot" of the Concord Stage.

"The boot" was the place where the driver sat perched in front. It was big enough to hold two passengers besides the driver; and a thousand pounds or more of mail could be packed in "the boot" also. Behind this was the body of the coach, big enough to hold six passengers. They sat three on each seat facing one another. It was hard on those not used to it to sit day and night through clouds of alkali dust or sand, through rain and slush, or snow and cold, cramped up in that stage. If we had to crowd more than six in, as we did occasionally, it was rather rough riding. When few passengers were along, or the mail was lighter, we made up our load with grain or other provisions to be distributed along at the various stations. So we were nearly always well loaded. Often we carried more than a ton of mail in "the boot," and strapped on the back platform.

Some pictures I have seen of the Overland Stage have passengers on top. This is a mistake. There was no place on the rounded top for passengers. Some of the boys occasionally lashed packages there. The passengers would have had to be strapped on too, if they had tried the top, for they would have got pitched off in a hurry, the stage rocked so. The body of the stage was hung on great leather springs, and it swung with a kind of cradle motion as we dashed along. When a fellow learned how to swing with it, things went all right; if he didn't, it was hard riding.

The road was not only rough and wearisome; it was dangerous. For a time the Indians were so troublesome that a soldier was sent with every stage. We should have felt safer without these soldiers though, for we knew how the Indians hated soldiers. The worst danger however, was not from Indians; they got lots of blame that didn't belong to them. It was the "road agents" that infested the country during those days that gave us most trouble.

Many a time these desperadoes would hold up the stage on some lonely place on the road. They would spring out before the horses and order the driver to stop or shoot down a horse to stop the stage; then after robbing the passengers and rifling the mail bags of their valuables, they would dash away with their plunder to their hiding places in the hills.

Some drivers, when these outlaws came upon them, would put the whip to their horses and try to dash by them to safety. At times the boys managed to give the robbers the slip, but oftener the driver would be shot down in the attempt to escape. Then the horses, mad with fright, if no passenger was aboard to grab the lines, would run away, upset the coach, perhaps, and string things along the trail in great shape. Sometimes they have dashed into a station with nothing but the front wheels dragging behind them.

I was lucky enough to escape such mishaps. The robbers never held me up; but one day I did have one of my wheel horses shot down, by some skulking desperado or Indian, we never knew which. I was swinging along a dugway down hill about two miles west of Canyon station when it happened. Three passengers — two men and a woman—were in the stage. All of a sudden my off wheel horse dropped dead.

I flung off the brake, knowing what was up, cracked my whip and way we went plunging down the hill, dragging the dead horse with us till I thought we were out of gunshot. No more shots came, so I stopped the team, jumped down and began to unhitch. The man inside the coach jumped out too, but instead of helping me, he grabbed the whip and began to lash the team, yelling to me to go on. He was so scared he acted like a crazy man till his wife jumped out, grabbed the whip from his hand and told him to behave himself. Then he cooled down a little; and with the help of the other passenger, I got the dead horse out of the harness, hitched one of the leaders in his place, and drove on to the next station, without any more trouble. I never found out who did that devilish trick, but I don't believe it was stage robbers, though, for they would have followed us up and finished their mischief. But other drivers were not so lucky. Three different times Major Egan brought in the stage with the driver dead in the boot and the stage shot full of holes. At one time a driver who had been wounded by outlaws, was loaded into my stage. We were trying to get him through to Salt Lake, but the poor fellow died while he was with me. No other passenger was along at the time. I couldn't help the sufferer much. It was a terrible experience, I tell you, for him and me too, that long night on the lonely Nevada desert.

Afterwards I was changed to another division, driving in Nevada from Austin to Sand Wells. Jim Clift was division agent here. It was a heavy road—full of sand; but it wasn't so hard and heavy an another stretch that Ben Holloday, our big chief, gave me later. When he heard I was careful with the horses, that I didn't use them up as did some of the drivers, they brought in from the East, who didn't know mountain life, he set me to driving from the sink of Carson to Fort Churchill. I drove there that summer and winter, and the next spring I was sent to drive from Carson City to Virginia City, Nevada.

I arrived at Carson City about ten o'clock one very fine morning in June. The mail agent met me just as I entered the town, and told me to drive to Tim Smith's big rock stable and put up my horses. He told me that the line I was driving on was in dispute, and he would have to go to Salt Lake City to see who had the right of way. "Stay here until you hear from me," he said, "and board in that hotel across the street." With that he left me alone, seven hundred miles from home and among strangers. If he had left me in an Indian camp, I should have felt all right, but to left away out there among a lot of hostile Gentiles, was more than I could bear.

I put my horses up, and while I was sitting out by the side of the stable, I saw a man come out of the hotel. He had on a white cap and a white apron that reached from his chin to his feet. In each hand he had a big, round, brass thing. He pounded these together and made a fearful racket. I had never seen a hotel before, to say nothing of being in one, and as the men that worked in the barn came rushing past me, I asked one of them what was up. "Dinner," he said. I got up and went over to the hotel, and when I went in, I never saw such a sight before. They had tables all over the house, and people were rushing in and sitting down to them.

I slipped in and took off my hat and stood by the side of the door waiting for some one to come up and ask me to sit down at a table, but nobody came. I stood there a while longer, and saw others come in and sit down at the tables without being asked, so I went sneaking up to a table and stood there, and as nobody asked me to sit down, I sat down anyhow. A waiter came up and began to mutter something to me. I said, "What?" He got it off again. I told him that I did not know what he said, so he went out and brought me something to eat. Just then a big, black-looking fellow came in and sat down on the opposite side of my table. A man that was sitting close by me said to him, "Well, Jack, I hear that you have enlisted." "Yes, sir," said Jack. "Where are you going?" "I am going to Salt Lake." "What are you going to do there?" "I am going to cut the heart out of the first Mormon I come across." Well, sir, that finished my dinner. Just as he said that, I was taking a drink of coffee, and it all went down my Sunday throat and very nearly choked me to death before I could get away from the table. I decided right there I wouldn't let anyone in Carson know I was a Mormon.

I went over to the stable and sat down, and then I began thinking of home. I didn't go back to the hotel that night for any supper, and when I went to bed, the fleas turned loose on me and I thought they would eat what was left of me before morning. You may talk about the persecutions of Nauvoo, but they couldn't be compared with my misery and woe at that time. I didn't sleep a wink that night, and when morning came I was hungry, sleepy, tired, and homesick.

When the man with the white cap and apron came out that morning with his brass plates and began to make another racket with them, I went over and walked right in, and turned around and walked right out again. I met one of the stable men and he asked me if I had been to breakfast. I said I had not. He said, "Come on in," and took me by the arm and we went in and sat down at a table. The waiter came up and got off the same thing that he said the day before, and the man that was with me told him to fetch it along. I told the waiter to bring me the same. Well, I ate two or three breakfasts that morning to make up for what I had lost, and then I felt very much better.

After breakfast we went back to the stable, and pretty soon Tim Smith came in and said, "Young man, it may be three weeks before the right of way is settled, but if you want to go to work in the stable I will give you three dollars a day." I agreed and began to work.

Tim Smith was a one-armed man, and he had fourteen hostlers and a clerk that worked in the stable. The office was in one corner of the stable and a young man by the name of Billy Green was the clerk. He had charge of the men and was very kind and good to me.

I was afraid to go out at night, so I stayed in the stable and helped Billy. It was a very large stable, holding over one hundred horses, and there was a good deal of work to do after dark. One night Mr. Smith was in the stable talking to Billy, and I heard him say, "That Mormon is as good a hand as you have here, isn't he?" "He is the best man we ever had here," replied Billy. I wondered how in thunder he knew I was a Mormon.

During the next day or two, first one and then another would ask how things were in Salt Lake. One day I asked one of them how he knew I was from Salt Lake. "Everybody in the town knows that you are a Mormon;" he said, "I know lots of Mormons, and I like them first rate." "Do all of the Gentiles think that way?" I asked him. He said most of them did. Then I told him what that black jack in the hotel, had said. He laughed, and said the fellow was just bragging, and if I had stepped up to him and told him I was a Mormon, it would have scared him to death.

After I found out that everyone knew I was a Mormon and none had hurt me yet, I began to get brave. Since that time I have been in a good many rough places, but I have never since tried to hide my religion. It doesn't pay.

At that time Virginia City was booming. Two or three men were killed every day. I had not driven here very long before I saw a man hanged at what they called Golden Gate. I don't remember what he had done, but I saw him hanged, anyway.

Those were rough, wild days, and this was one

of the roughest spots in the savage West. I was glad enough to leave it. After a few months of staging here, I quit the job and returned home.

CHAPTER XVIII.

A TERRIBLE JOURNEY.

When I returned from Nevada to Utah, I found that Mother had moved to Cache Valley, so I went up there and stayed all winter with her. It proved to be a very sad winter for me, though it began very happily. I found here my first sweetheart, a beautiful girl, who made me love her very dearly by her sweet ways and her kind heart; for she helped my mother nurse me through a dangerous illness.

We had spent the time delightfully for about a month, when I got hurt. My horse, which I was riding one day very fast, struck some ice, slipped and fell, throwing me to the ground. My head struck the ice so hard that it nearly killed me. I was carried home; brain fever came on and I lay in bed till spring. To make matters worse, the wound in my head broke out again and I was delirious for part of the time. But this dear girl stayed by my bedside day after day, and helped me past death's door. They thought I was dying one day and she was driven half wild for fear I might go; but the next day I had rallied and from then on I recovered very fast.

Our intention was to get married; but before we could realize our hopes they were blighted and destroyed by certain men who should have been our friends. These men poisoned the minds of her parents against me, while I was away driving the stage and guarding the cattle of the people against the Indians; her parents refused to allow her to answer my letters; and finally they succeeded in making her give me up and marry one of the men who had turned them against me.

We were both heart-broken. She told me afterwards how she was driven to do it. I could not blame her; but I do blame those who wrought upon her in an underhanded way, and so shocked my faith in men as almost to embitter me for life. Thanks, however, to my dear mother, my other kind friends, and to my Heavenly Father, I have been able to live down that bitterness, and meet not only this, but many other sore trials that have come to me, with courage enough to master them. This trial at least taught me to place my trust in God, more than in man.

The little bunch of cattle, which I had bought with the money I had received for my team, were stolen that winter, presumably by the Indians. I hunted for them for a while but not one did I ever get back. The money I had saved for a "wedding stake," I gave to mother; and as I had no heart to stay in that town any longer, I started for the road again.

That summer I worked for John Bolwinkle of Salt Lake City, as his wagon boss, in charge of his ox-train freighting from Carson City, Nevada, A mail route had been established from Salt Lake City to Bannock, Montana, and Mr. Leonard I. Smith, obtained the contract to carry this mail. Knowing of my experience in this business, he induced me to drive the stage from Salt Lake north that winter.

We started out some time in November with a wagon load of dry goods to trade for horses along the road. Besides this, we had one light coach and two buggies, in which were seven passengers. We went on our journey through Ogden, Brigham City, and other towns north, buying what horses we could as we went along. For a few days we stopped at Soda Springs to arrange about making a mail station there. At that time a large company of soldiers were wintering in the town.

It was the plan of Mr. Smith to make me division agent from Soda Springs to Salt Lake but I was to go on with him to Bannock to get acquainted with the whole route.

When we got to Bannock, winter had set in. It snowed very hard while we were there, and kept snowing all of the way back. By the time we got to Snake River, the snow was deep, and there was no place where we could buy feed for our horses. We had two passengers with us, and Mr. Smith had not provided us with supplies enough to last us half way back to Soda Springs.

We could not travel as fast as he had planned on account of the deep snow, and the horses were getting very weak for want of food. For these reasons we could not come back on the road we had taken going, so we kept down the Snake River to where the Blackfoot empties into it. There we ate the last of our provisions. We were still one hundred miles from any place where we could get more, and the snow was becoming deeper every day. When we got up the Ross Fork canyon we had to stop for the night. Here three of the horses gave out, and we had to leave them and one of the buggies. We had left the coach at Beaver Canyon.

The next morning we started before breakfast, for we had eaten the last thing the morning before. The snow kept falling all the time, and by non, it was at least three feet deep. All of us but the driver would walk ahead of the team to break the road. We had four horses on the buggy, and it would push up the snow ahead of it until it would run into the buggy over the dash-board and sides. That day two more of the horses gave out and we had to leave them, but we reached the head of the Portneuf.

That night we all turned out and kicked the snow off of a little space so the poor horses could get some frozen grass, but it was so very cold and they were so tired that they would not eat very much.

The next morning we made another early start, and Mr. Smith said we would get to Soda Springs that day, but I knew we could not get there that day, nor the next day, either. I told the passengers that if we were to leave the buggy, we might make it in two days, but the way we were fooling along with the worn-out horses, we never would get there. They told Mr. Smith what I said and he upbraided me for it. He said I had scared the passengers nearly to death and he wanted me to stop it.

Well, by noon that day we came to the road
we had come out on, but Mr. Smith did not know
the place and wanted to follow the road over which
we had traveled in going to Bannock. I told him
the way we wanted to go was south, but the way
he wanted to go was north. He told me I was
wrong and ordered me to keep still. I said, ''I
will go to Soda Springs and you can go to the
other place,'' so I took what I wanted out of the
buggy and started off, but I had not gone far
when I heard some one calling me. It was so
foggy and the frost was falling so fast that I could
see only a few yards and as I hesitated about going back, one of the passengers came up to me
and asked me if I was sure I knew where I was
going, and begged me to come back to the buggy.

One of the passengers was a large, strong
Irishman, and appeared to be well educated; the
other was a sickly looking Englishman. I don't
remember their names, but they called each other
Mike and Jimmy. I went back to the buggy and
Mike saw that I did not want anything to say to
Mr. Smith, so he did the talking. He questioned
Mr. Smith and then me for quite a while, and then
he said he believed that I was right. He told the
driver to turn the team around and follow me. The

driver obeyed although it made Mr. Smith very angry.

After turning south we had not traveled over four miles, when one of the remaining horses gave out and we could not get the poor thing to move, so we had to leave the buggy. We went on about three or four hundred yards to a clump of quaking asp, and built a large fire. When we all got warm, I went to bring up the horses and buggy and when I got back to the fire, Mr. Smith and Mike were quarreling. Mr. Smith said that we were going away from Soda Springs, and that he intended to turn and go the other way.

It was already quite dark, but we could travel just as well in the night as in the day, for we could not see very far anyhow on account of the fog. I said I knew I was right and for all those who wanted to go to Soda Springs to fall in line, for I was going to start right then. I went to the buggy and got a pair of buffalo moccasins I had there, put them on, and started down the trail. Mike said, ''Hold on, I will go with you.'' Then Jimmy said he was not going to stay there and starve to death, that he would go with us, too. So the three of us went our way and left Mr. Smith and the driver standing there in the fog and snow.

It was about eleven o'clock at night when we left the buggy, and we did not feel much like pushing our way through the snow, for we had already walked many miles that day, and had been three days without anything to eat. Mike said he would take the lead to break the path, I was to come next, and Jimmy was to follow me. There was about a foot of snow with a crust on it, not quite hard enough to hold one up, and on top of this was about two feet of frost, so you see it was very hard traveling.

We had not been out over two hours, when Mike said his feet were frozen. I had a few matches in my pocket wrapped up in paper, and we kicked around to find some dry sagebrush, but it was all wet and frozen. We broke up some and tried to make a fire, but it would not burn. Pretty soon Mike said to give him the matches and he would try it. He took them and laid them down by his side while trying to light one, and Jimmy came up, struck them with his foot, and scattered them all through the snow. We could not find a single one of them, so we had to go without any fire.

We trudged along, stumbling over sagebrush and rock until morning. Mike said we must be very near Soda Springs, for he thought we had traveled twenty miles or more during the night, and he could not believe me when I told him we had not made over eight miles. I told them before we left the buggy that it was about thirty miles to Soda Springs, so I knew we had over twenty miles yet.

Jimmy and I were about played out, and had to stop every little while to rest. Mike had long legs, but Jimmy and I were so short that when we tried to step in his tracks we had to jump, and that made it harder for Jimmy and me. During the night we had traveled too far to the east and had left the trail through the lava beds and sagebrush, and had started to cross the big meadow and swamps along the Blackfoot River. The tall slough grass and bulrushes were so tangled and frozen together that we could hardly get through them. Somehimes Mike would forget himself and step about six feet over a large mass of grass and rushes, and Jimmy and I would have to wallow through them.

About noon the fog rose a little and we could see a large butte which we called the Chinaman's Hat, and which I knew was twelve miles from Soda Springs. The butte was about four miles ahead of us, which would make it sixteen miles from where we were to Soda. Jimmy said his feet were frozen, and that he was too tired to go much farther. I was about worn out, too, so we were in a pretty bad fix. The fog soon settled again, and was so thick that we could not see fifty yards, and we were all so tired out that I knew we could not reach the Chinaman's Hat before ten o'clock that night.

We decided that we must not stop to rest more than ten minutes at any time, and that at least one of us must keep awake, for we knew that if all went to sleep at the same time we would never again wake up.

It was a bitter cold night. There was no wind blowing, and it was very still, not even a bird, rabbit, or coyote was to be seen or heard—not a sound but the ringing in our ears. By this time I had gotten over my being hungry, but I was very thirsty, and I had eaten so much frost to satisfy my thirst that my mouth and tongue had become so sore and swollen that I could scarcely speak. Jimmy was so used up by this time that we could hardly get him to move after we had stopped to rest, and Mike would sometimes carry him a little ways, but Jimmy said it hurt him, so Mike would have to put him down.

Well, night was coming on again, and I do not think we had traveled over three or four miles that day, but we were doing the best we could. About four o'clock in the afternoon we stopped for a few minutes' rest, I settled back in the snow and put one foot out for Jimmy to lay his head on. Soon it was time to start again and I shook Jimmy, but he did not stir. Mike had already started, so I pulled my foot out from under Jimmy's head, and as I did so his head sank in the snow. Then I took hold of him and tried to raise him, but I could not. I called for Mike, and when he came back, we raised Jimmy up, and I saw that he was dead.

I cannot tell you what happened in the next half hour, but from what he said in his sorrow over Jimmy's death, I learned for the first time that Jimmy had married Mike's sister. After a while I scraped the snow away clear to the ground, and while doing this, I found a dry thistle stalk about fourteen inches long. I took the dead man's coat off, laid him in the hole, spread the coat over his face, and covered him with snow, making a little mound like a grave. I tore some of the lining from my coat, tied it to the thistle, and stuck it over the grave.

It was hard work to get Mike started again. He said we were all going to die anyway, and he would rather stay there with Jimmy. I told him we were nearly to Soda Springs, and if he would try, we could get there; but he said I had told him that so much that he didn't believe I knew where Soda Springs was. He said I had told him when we first started from the buggy that it was only thirty miles and he knew we had traveled over seventy miles by this time. I told him I knew if we traveled as fast as we could that we would be in Soda Springs in two hours.

We talked there a long time, and I began to think that Mike had really made up his mind not to try to go on any more, when just before dark he seemed to take fresh courage. He jumped up and started out so fast that I could not keep up with him. After a little while he stopped and sat down again in the snow, and when I caught up to him I found him sound asleep. I let the poorfellow sleep a few minutes, and then I found it almost impossible to wake him. After pulling and shaking him, I finally got him on his feet, but he would start off the wrong way. Then I would get hold of him and start him off right, but he would turn around and go the wrong way. He did not know what he was doing, so I had to take the lead. Then he would stop and I would have to go back and get him.

After a little time he seemed to come to himself, and took the lead again for about a mile, and then he sat down in the snow and said he was done for, and that he would not go another step. I did all I could to rouse him but he would not stir. He gave me a small memorandum book and a little buckskin bag full of gold dust, and told me he had a sister living in Mississippi, and that I would find her address in the book. I talked to him a long time to try to get him to come with me, but he would not move.

I saw that it was of no use, and that I would have to leave him or lie down in the snow and die with him. This I felt like doing, but for the sake of my mother and sisters, I thought I would make one more effort to reach the town, so I left him and had gone about seventy-five yards, when I stumbled over something and fell headlong into the snow. I cleared the snow away from my face, and sat there thinking about home and how badly my mother would feel if she knew where I was, and how easy it would be to lie there in the snow and go to sleep.

Drowsiness had nearly overcome me when, suddenly, I heard the faraway tinkle of a bell. I knew then that I was not far from Soda Springs. I jumped up and ran back to Mike as fast as I could go, and when I got to him, I found him stretched out on the snow with his hands folded over his breast and sound asleep. It was all but impossible to wake him. I am certain he would have died if he had been left ten minutes longer. When I got him awake enough to tell him about the bell, the sound had ceased. He would not believe what I told him about it so I could not get him to come with me.

I went back to the place where I first heard the bell and sat down again. In a few minutes I heard it louder than before. Then I rushed back to Mike and found him awake and when I got him to listen, he heard the bell this time, too. He jumped up and started so fast in the direction of the sound that I could not keep up with him. When he would see me falling behind, he would come back and take hold of my hands and pull me along. I begged him to let me alone and told him it hurt me to be jerked over the snow in that way. Then he would kick the snow and say that he would make a good road for me if I would only come.

We had traveled this way for about half an hour, when the fog rose a little and we saw, a short distance ahead of us, a faint light. He then left me and started for the light as fast as he could go. I tried to follow, but slipped and fell, and found that I could not get up again. Many times I tried to rise, but fell back every time. I thought if I lay there a while and rested, then perhaps I could get up and go on. I guess I must have fallen asleep, for the first thing I knew, two men had hold of me and were carrying me to the hotel where we had seen the light. Mike had reached there and had told the men in the hotel that one of his companions was dead and another was out there just a little ways dying in the snow.

When we got to the door, Mike was standing there with a big glass of whiskey in his hand. He said, ''Down this, old boy, and it will be the making of you,'' but I could not bear the smell of liquor, to say nothing of drinking it.

They set me down in a chair near the stove, but the heat soon made me feel sick and I had to move as far from the fire as I could get. The cook brought something for us to eat, but my mouth and tongue hurt me so that I could hardly eat anything. Then the light began to grow dim and I could feel them shaking me and could hear them talking to me, but I could not answer for my tongue was so swollen. Then I seemed to go away off.

The next thing I remember, they were tellling

me that the doctors had come, and I saw that the house was full of people. They told me Mike's feet were frozen and that two men were holding them in a tub of cold water to try to draw the frost out. The doctor was pulling my moccasins off and I heard him say that my feet were all right. It seems that they were giving me hot soup or something every minute, but I was so sleepy that I hardly knew what was going on. I soon found myself in bed with two doctors standing over me. One of them was the faithful Doctor Palmer who, years afterwards, became a dear friend and neighbor of mine. He told me they had just brought in the dead man, and that they did not know what to do with him until either Mike or I was able to talk. They were going to hold an inquest over the body and wanted witnesses to tell how he died. I tried to ask if they had sent for Mr. Smith, but they could not understand what I said.

I don't know how much time had passed, when an army officer came in and began talking to Doctor Palmer. I heard Doctor Palmer say, "Is that so?" The officer said it was. Then Doctor Palmer said, "My God! I did not know he was that bad." I rose to ask what was the matter, but Doctor Palmer told me to lie still. The officer said, "Shall

I tell him?'' Doctor Palmer said, ''Not now, let the other doctor tell him.'' The officer went out and soon the old doctor came in. He told me that the man who came with me had his feet so badly frozen that he could not save them and they would have to be taken off. He said he would leave Sergeant Chauncey with me while Doctor Palmer assisted him in cutting off Mike's feet. He told me to keep very quiet and in a few days I would be all right.

About two hours after Mike and I reached the hotel, a company of men started out to find Mr. Smith; and when they reached the buggy, they found Mr. Smith and the driver all right. They had the meat of two horses cut up and hanging in the trees. When they told Mr. Smith that Mike and I had reached Soda Springs but that Jimmy was dead, he said he was surprised that we were not all dead, for he was certain that I was leading them right away from the town.

The party that went out for Mr. Smith got back the day the doctors were going to cut Mike's feet off. Mr. Smith came in to see me, and he almost cried when he saw the fix I was in. He said he would take me right to Salt Lake City, where I would get better care than I could in Soda

Springs They would not allow him to move me, however, though he tried his hardest to take me.

Owing to the skill of Doctor Palmer I got along pretty well, but it was several weeks before I was able to get around very much. Poor Mike suffered terribly after his feet were taken off, but he got well and strong as ever, except for the loss of his feet.

When I got well, I drove the mail from Soda Springs to Franklin during the rest of the winter. That June Jimmy's wife came out from Mississippi. She was Mike's sister, and the most beautiful woman I ever saw.

She and Mike induced me to stop driving the mail for a while and take them back over the road we traveled those awful days to reach Soda Springs. I secured a buggy for us to ride in, a small spring wagon to carry the camp outfit, and a good cook to go with us to do the cooking and drive the mess wagon.

We first stopped where Jimmy died. The spot was still marked by the pieces of my coat lining that were lying aronud. Then we went to where we had left Mr. Smith and his driver. When we reached the place where Mr. Smith wanted to turn north and follow the old trail in the wrong direc-

Elk that Were Being Hotly Pursued

tion, Mike told his sister that if it had not been for me that day, they would all have gone the wrong way and there, somewhere on that lonely trail, have perished in the snow. From there we went to the Snake River, where we had eaten our last meal on that awful trip.

We found here a large band of Indians, and among them were several that I was acquainted with. We could not get away from them, they were so glad to see me, so we stayed here four days. They wanted to know why I didn't come back in those days and live with them all the time. Then I had to tell them all about where I had been ever since I went away from them and what I had been doing all that time. They took turns asking me questions until I thought they would talk me to death.

These were the first Indians this woman had ever seen, and she was frightened of them until she noticed how glad they were to see me and how kind they were then she felt better towards them. She said she was delighted to hear me talk to them, that they were certainly a queer people, and that I must have been a strange boy to leave my home and go to live with them.

After I had finished my visit with the Indians

we returned over the same road. When we got back to mother's home Mike and his sister stayed with us three weeks. They kept trying all the time to induce me to go with them to her home in Mississippi, but my mother objected so strongly that I would not go, although I wanted to very much. They would have treated me very kindly, I am sure. They even offered to share their property with me; but I thought more of my mother than I did of any body else in the world and I could not leave her to make my home among strangers.

MY OLD SHOSHONE FRIENDS.

"What became of your old Indian friends, your mother, Washakie, Hanabi, and the rest?" This question has been asked me again and again. "Did you ever see them?" "What other experiences did you have with the Indians." Such queries as these have been sent to me from even far off France by people who have read the first edition of my little book.

To satisfy my readers on these points and others that may be of interest I have added a few more chapters to my story.

When I left my dear old Indian mother up north on "Pohogoy," or Ross Fork,—a place near the Snake River, I promised her I would come back to her. That promise I intended to keep; but I was prevented from doing so by other pressing duties, till it was too late.

She waited a year for her "Yagaiki" to return, then her sorrow became so great she couldn't bear it longer and she started out to hunt me up. The Indians told me later that after I had been gone a few months my old mother would roam off in the mountains and lonely places and stay until hunger would drive her home. Finally she came to my white mother's home in Grantsville to find her boy. My mother made her welcome, taking my Indian mother into her home, feeding her, and providing her with a room as one of the family.

Then she wrote me that my two mothers wanted me to come home. I wished with all my heart to do so, but at that time I was about five hundred miles away, out on the mail line, badly wounded in the head by an Indian arrow. When I recovered enough to travel, I had to go to work again. The Indians at this time were burning stations and killing men every chance they got. Riders became so scarce and hard to get that I could not well leave, no matter how I felt.

When I finally did get away, I found that my

own mother, as I have said before, had moved into Cache Valley, and my old Indian mother had left her, broken hearted because she had not found her papoose. She had stayed with my white mother for more than two months. When I did not return as she expected, she grew suspicious that my white mother had hidden me away; and no words could comfort her or change her mind. Finally she went off with some Indians who came there.

My mother urged me to hunt her up. She had taken quite a fancy to the Indian woman. She thought it my duty to find and care for her the rest of her life. I felt so too. She had been a dear friend to me. She had cared for me and protected me from harm, even saving my life several times.

Another little incident I call up as I think of her shows her solicitude for me. One night when I was among the Shoshones as a boy I was playing with the Indian boys. The game was killing whitemen. We had our bows and arrows and were slipping up to bunches of brush and shooting at them. Whenever we clipped a twig from the bushes, that was a scalp. We would stick it in our belts and strut about like big ''Injuns.'' In the midst of our fun my mother called — ''Yagaiki, kem a

yup way a,'' which meant "Come in and go to bed."
As I paid no attention she kept on calling and
coming closer till she stood by me and said: "Hag-
ani-in-a-kakim, so-can-ne-a-tagum," "Why didn't
you come when I called you?"

"Ne-a-ka-meak senape?", I answered sulkily,
which meant, "I don't want to go to bed." With
that she grabbed me by the collar, and suddenly I
found myself being half jerked, half shoved towards
the wigwam. I begged and promised, but it was
no use. She wouldn't let go till, within the tent
she flung me forward on a pile of blankets.

"Washakie," she said to her son, the chief,
who was sitting in the wigwam, "You must do
something with this boy; he won't mind me." With
that she left and I heard her crying outside.

The chief looked at me a moment and said
quietly: "What is the trouble between you and
mother?" "Well, she won't let me play; she makes
me come in every night before dark. The other
boys stay out; I don't see why I can't," I answered.

"Mother knows why," he replied. "You
should be good to mother; she is good to you—better than she ever was to me."

Mother had come in again by this time. "You
must not stay out after dark," she told me. "Those

papooses would just as soon kill you as not. They have been trained to think it is an honor to kill a white man. If they could do it without being caught, they might put an arrow through you any minute. I know what is best for you, Yagaiki. You must come when I call.''

I always did after that.

The next word I got of my Indian mother was that she was dead. This sad news came from a band of Shoshones I found in the Bear Lake valley. Hearing they were there, I had gone to see them, thinking to meet some of my old Indian friends. But those I wished most to see were not among the band. My dear old mother, they told me, had died about three years after I left. Washakie was then out in the Wind River country. As these Indians were going there, I decided to go with them.

We found Washakie at South Pass. He was very glad to see me, treated me like a brother. But he could not tell me just where our mother was buried, as he had happened to be away from her when she died. He only knew that her grave was somewhere on Ham's Fork. We found an Indian who said he knew where it was. I offered to give him a pony if he would guide me to it. He agreed, and we went back to the head of Ham's Fork. We found the camping place they were at when she died, but not the grave, though we hunted for three days together, and I stayed another day after he left. Since then I have passed the place many times and have searched again and again; for I did desire to carry out my old Indian mother's wish to be buried like the whites, but I have never found her grave.

It was the custom of the Indians to bury their dead in some cleft or rocks or wash. They left no mark over the grave, but they usually buried with the body articles the deceased had treasured in life, as weapons, clothing,etc. In the grave with my dear old mother they placed the beaded and tasseled quiver she had made of the skin of the antelope I had killed, the auger I had sent to Salt Lake for, and other things of mine she had kept after I went away. There are those who think an Indian has no heart. This dear old lady certainly had one that was tender and true. Her soul was good and pure. Peace to her memory.

Washakie's wife Hanabi was another good woman. She, too, had died before I returned to the Indians. Her little girl papoose, the baby when I was with them, grew up, I have been told, and married.

Washakie married another squaw by whom he had several children. One of them, Dick Washakie, is still living in the Wind River country. He is a wealthy Indian, and has considerable influence.

When these Shoshone Indians made their treaty with the Government there were three reservations set apart for the Shoshone tribe—Fort Hall, Lemhi, and Wind River. Washakie was given his choice. He took the Wind River reserve because, as he told me afterwards, it had been his boyhood home, and his father was buried there. Here Washakie spent the rest of his life honored by his tribe, and respected for his goodness and his wisdom by all the whites who knew him. During the early nineties he passed to the Happy Hunting Grounds.

I saw Washakie many times before he died. We were always brothers. When I lived in Bloomington, Bear Lake Country, Idaho, Washakie often came and stayed with me. He was always made welcome in my home, and his lodge was always open to me. During the time of Chief Joseph's war, Washakie brought his band and camped for some months near my ranch on Bear River: and every day he would come to get the news of the war. My wife would read the paper and I would interpret it for the Indians.

While this war was on, the whites would not sell ammunition to the Indians without a letter of recommendation, or "Tabop," as they called it. The Indians all came to me for these letters. My home for years was their headquarters. They would have eaten me out of house and home, if the ward authorities had not come to my rescue and helped to feed these Red brethren.

TRAPPING WITH AN INDIAN.

But the Indians were not always a burden. They sometimes gave me good help. At one time in particular, I found an Indian who proved a friend in need. It was during the winter of 1866-7, the year after I had brought my wife from Oxford, Idaho, to Bloomington.

"Hogitsi," a Shoshone Indian, with his family was wintering in the town at the time. The whites called him "Hog," but he hadn't a bit of the hog in his nature. I found him to be one of the best Indians I ever knew.

After I had got well acquainted with him, he proposed that we try trapping to make some money. I was hard up; my family was destitute of food and clothing, for I had hard luck that summer, so I was ready to try anything.

We set to work over in Nounan valley on a little stream about fifteen miles from home. The results were very encouraging. At the end of the first week we came back with sixty dollars worth of furs. It was the easiest money I ever made in my life. Such success made us ready to try again.

"Hog" proposed that we go down to the Port Neuf country and spend the winter at the trapping business. He said he knew of a stream there that was full of beaver and mink and other fur animals. I was anxious to go but my wife protested that she could not think of my going off for a whole winter with an Indian. She was sure I would be scalped. It was hard work for me to persuade her that under our circumstances it was the right thing to do. She finally consented, however, and we set to work to get ready.

With "Hog" to help we soon had enough winter's wood chopped up to last my family through the winter. I did all I could otherwise to leave them comfortable; but the best I could do was not enough to keep them from having a hard time of it while I was away.

I had three horses. Hog got two more from Thomas Rich; and Joseph Rich, who kept a store in Paris, supplied us with provisions and camp outfit upon our agreeing to sell to him what furs we should get.

It was about a week after New Years that we struck out northward through the cold and snow. The snow got deeper and deeper as we went on towards Soda Springs. It seemed impossible to make our destination. I suggested that we turn back, but "Hog" wouldn't listen to me. He said that we would find the snow lighter from there on, and it would be only a day or two more before we got to the Port Neuf. So I yielded and we pushed on till we reached Dempsey Creek, a branch of the Port Neuf. Here we made our winter camp at the base of the lava cliffs that border the stream near where it empties into the Port Neuf. We chose a good place on the sunny side of the rock, and built our quarters. A cleft up the face of the cliff served us well. By building up a fourth side to this cleft, we made a fine chimney and fire place. Around this we made our shack—of quaking asp poles and willows, and long grass to thatch it. For a door we used the skins of two white tailed deer stretched over a quaking asp frame. Our house was a cosy shelter from the storms, and roomy enough to store our bales of furs. For wood we used cedar, which grew nearby.

Within the cedars we found plenty of black tail deer, while in the willows the white-tail were so numerous that we had little trouble to get all we needed. Trout we could catch at any time: so we had food in abundance.

When it came to trapping, we found beaver and mink so thick that it was no trick at all to catch them. Otter were not so plentiful, but we did land several of these beautiful animals.

I tended the traps and did the cooking. Hogitsi skinned the animals, stretched the fur and kept watch of the horses. He was a good worker—not a lazy thing about him. Usually he was in bed an hour before me, and up an hour earlier. By the time I was ready to tumble out, he had the fire roaring and was at work on the skins. While I got breakfast, he would look after the horses, and bring my old buckskin mare to camp. After breakfast I would get on her and ride the rounds of the traps to see what luck the night had brought. Usually I found the traps all sprung and a beaver or mink or sometimes an otter in them, tail up, and drowned in the stream. For we weighted the traps with a rock to hold the animal when caught, under water. If the animal is not drowned, he will often gnaw off his foot and get away. After taking out the game,

I would reset the traps, and return to camp with my load.

To keep the traps going, kept me busy all day. We caught animals so fast that I had some times to stop and help Hogitsi catch up with his skinning and stretching. We would sit up at times late at night at this work. Evidently little trapping, if any, had ever been done on this stream, for the animals seemed not to know what a trap meant.

If it hadn't been for the worry I had for my dear ones at home, the winter would have been a pleasant one in every way. It was one of the easiest I ever spent, and most profitable. I never have made money faster than I did that winter. When spring time came, we had about seven hundred pounds of fur. At that time mink and beaver skins sold at two dollars per pound; otter was worth one dollar a foot. A stretched otter skin would often bring nine dollars or more.

When we turned over our pack to Mr. Rich, we found we had $900.00 due us after paying all our expenses. He paid us in gold, silver, and greenbacks. Hogitsi was scared when he saw the pile; and when it came to dividing, he certainly proved that he was no "Hog;" for he simply would not take his full share. He insisted that we should not have had any if it hadn't been for me; that it would "make him too rich."

This streak of good luck gave me a new start. My wife felt better about the trapping business; but she had no desire to repeat the experiences of that winter; and, as I found other profitable work to do, I did not turn to trapping again as a business, though I have done a good deal of this work at various times since. And I have also done a good deal of trading in furs with the trappers.

This trading has brought me into acquaintanceship with a good many of the mountaineers. It was through this that I came to know Kit Carson, who came to my home hunting his trapper. son-in-law, Sims, one winter. Sims was wintering near at the time. He stopped over night with me. I brought Kit's son-in-law to my home and they made up their troubles. Kit wanted to stay with me for a while. I took him in, and we boarded and lodged him for several months. We had a good time together swapping yarns that winter I can tell you.

When the Government undertook the task of settling the Indians on the reservations, I was given the job of helping the Indian Agent of the Fort Hall reservation gather and keep the Redmen within bounds. This was no easy task. The Indians

found it hard, after their many years of roving life,
to be restrained. They often grew discontented,
complaining at times that they were being cheated
and otherwise mistreated. It is a well known fact
that they often had much cause to complain. The
Indians have been abused shamefully by the whites
at times, and I know it. Our dealings with the
Redmen reflect no great credit on us.

If the Indians became disgruntled, as they fre-
quently did, they would slip away to the mountains
in a sulky mood. Whenever they did this, it was
my business to bring them back. This task was
not disagreeable, but was sometimes dangerous.

At one time a band under the lead of old Sagwich, got angry over something, and struck for the
hills, strongly determined that they would not come
back to the reservation again.

I was sent to bring them back; they had a
week the start of me. I had a good horse, however,
and taking with me an Indian boy named Suarki,
to lead the pack horse, I started out. The second
day we struck their trail, and knowing well the
signs they always leave behind them, we followed
it easily; but it led us over a hundred and fifty
miles through a rough country before we found the
runaway band.

On the sixth day we came upon them camped on the Salmon River. We pitched our camp about a hundred yards away. After unsaddling our horses, I went over to have a talk with them.

Old Sagwich was very angry. He said he knew what I was after, but he wouldn't go back; and I would not go back either, for they would fix me so that I couldn't give them any more trouble. He said I ought to be their friend, but instead of that I was helping to bring more trouble to them. The whites he accused of lying to them and robbing them of their hunting ground and forcing them to work at something they knew nothing about. They would bear it no longer; they would fight first. The old chief grew angrier as he went on.

"You need not think of escaping this time," he said to me. "We intend to tie you to that tree and burn you alive." I tried to reason with them, telling them I knew I was in their power; but it wouldn't do them any good to kill me. If they did, the soldiers would soon follow and kill the last one of them.

"We are not afraid of the soldierrs," he retorted; "We would rather die fighting than starve."

"Well," I replied, "If you kill me, you will kill one of the best friends the Indians ever had."

Buffaloes

But nothing I could say seemed to make any difference with old Sagwich. He was determined to carry out his threat. If he had his way I knew he would do it. The other Indians, however, did not act so devilish. One of them gave me some fresh elk meat, and I went back to my camp. Things looked rather black for me that night. My only hope was that the other Indians would not stand by old Sagwich.

If the worst came, I had determined to sell my life as dearly as possible. The Indians held a council that night. We kept close watch till morning, but as no one offered to harm us, we began to feel a little easier. After saddling our horses, I told Suarki I was going over to have another talk with them, and instructed him that if they made a move to kill me, he should leap on my horse and strike for home to tell the Indian Agent.

Old Sagwich was so sulky he wouldn't even speak to me. The other Indians, however, acted better. They said nothing of what had been decided, but that day they packed up and took the trail towards home. We followed them. On our way down the river we came upon one of the Indians fishing. He told me about the council. Old Sagwich was stubborn in his determination to kill me, but the rest wouldn't consent and he had to give up his bloody plan.

This experience made me feel that my job was too risky for the pay I was getting. The Agent wouldn't raise my wages, so I quit him and went back to my home at Oxford, Idaho.

FRONTIER TROUBLES.

Later, we moved back into the Bear Lake, where we made our home for twenty years. During this time I was often called on to do dangerous service in the interest of our settlements. After the Indian troubles were over, we had outlaws to deal with who were worse than Indians. For along time the frontier communities suffered from depredations committed by cattle-rustlers and horse thieves. Organized bands operated from Montana to Colorado. They had stations about a hundred miles apart in the roughest places in the mountains. They would often raid our ranges and steal all the cattle and horses they could pick up driving them into their mountain retreats. They got so daring finally that they even came into the settlements and robbed stores and killed men. The colonists did not get together to stop these outrages till after a fatal raid was made upon Montpelier, when a store was robbed and a clerk was shot dead. This roused the people of the valley to action. Gen. Chas. C. Rich called upon the bishops to send two men from each settlement — the best men to be had — to pursue and punish the outlaws. Fourteen men responded to the call, among them four of the bishops themselves. It fell to my lot to be one of this posse.

We struck across the mountains east of Bear Lake, following the trail of the robbers to their rendezvous on the Big Piney, a tributary of the Green River. We knew that they had hidden themselves in this country, for two of the men with us, whose stock had been stolen, had followed the robbers to their den to recover their property. Finding the outlaws in such force they didn't dare to claim their stolen stock but returned to Bear Lake for help.

These men led us to the place where they had come upon the outlaws; but the outlaws had evidently feared pursuit and moved camp. To hide their tracks they had driven their wagons up the creek right in the water for over a mile. Then they had left the creek and driven up a little ravine and over a ridge. As we rode up this ravine, to the top of the ridge, the two men who were in the lead sighted the wickiups of the robbers in the hollow below. They dodged back to keep out of sight and we all rode down into the thick willows on the Big Piney, hiding our horses and ourselves among them. The two men that had sighted the outlaw camp then slipped up the hill again on foot, and secreting themselves in the sage brush at the top of the ridge, watched the rest of the afternoon to see whether the outlaws had mistrusted anything; but they showed no sign of having seen us. At dark they came and reported.

We held council then to decide what plan to pursue to capture the outlaws. As the robbers outnumbered us, more than two to one, and were well armed, it was serious business. Our sheriff weakened when the test came; he said he couldn't do it; and turned his papers over to Joseph Rich, as brave a man as ever went on such a trip. There were others who felt pretty shaky and wanted to turn back, but Mr. Rich said we had been picked as the best men in Bear Lake and he didn't feel like going back without making an attempt to capture the thieving band. One man said he was ready to go cut the throats of the whole bunch of robbers if the captain said so, but Mr. Rich said, "No; we did not come out to shed blood. We want to take them alive and give them a fair trial."

Every man was given a chance to say how he

felt. Most of us wanted to make the attempt to capture the outlaws and the majority ruled.

How to do it was the next problem. It would have been folly for so few of us to make an open attack on so many well armed men. The only way we could take them was by surprise, when they were asleep. This plan agreed upon, Mr. Rich proposed that we go down the hill with our horses and pack animals, get in line at the bottom, then just at the peep of day, charge upon their camp, jump from our horses, run into their tents and grab their guns. When we had decided on this plan of action, Mr. Rich said that this probably meant a fight. If it did we should let them fire first. Should they kill one of us, we must not run; for if we did so they would kill us all. We should give them the best we had. With our double barreled shot guns loaded with buckshot, we would make things pretty hot for them if they showed fight.

In order that we might know exactly the situation, and have our tents picked out beforehand, so as not to get in a mix up, two volunteers were called for to go down through their camp in the night and get the lay of things. Johnathan Hoopes and I offered to go. Their wickiups were pitched on both sides of a little stream, which was deep enough for us to keep out of sight by stooping a little. Down this stream we stole our way, wading with the current so as not to make any noise, till we got right among the tepees. The biggest one was pitched on the brink of the stream. We could hear some of the men inside of it snoring away lustily. Hoopes reached his hand up and found a blanket on which were some service berries spread out to dry. Being hungry, we helped ourselves, filling our pockets with them. After taking in the situation fully, we slipped back to our boys.

There were seven tents in all, and fourteen of us—two to each tent. Hoopes and I were to take the largest, the other boys were assigned theirs. We waited for day to break; just as it did, the word was given; we popped spurs to our horses and away we went. A few seconds and we had leaped from them, rushed into the tents and begun to grab the guns from the robbers, who, waked so rudely, stared stupidly, while we gathered in their weapons. By the time Hoopes was through passing them out to me, I had my arms loaded with rifles and revolvers. Mr. Rich told me to carry them up the hill a piece and stack them. "Shoot the first man who makes a move to touch them," was his order. When I looked around, there sat three of our men on their horses, they hadn't done their duty; so some of the tents were yet untouched. I told Hoopes, and he jumped over the creek to one of them. I was just gathering up some weapons I had dropped when a big half-breed made a jump at me, grabbed my shot gun, and we had a lively tussle for a few minutes. He might have got the better of me, for he was a good deal bigger than I, but Hoopes jumped to the rescue and cracked him on the head with his revolver so hard that it knocked him senseless for some time.

When the outlaws rallied themselves enough to sense what had happened, they broke out of their tents in double quick time, swearing and cursing and demanding what we wanted.

Captain Rich told them to keep quiet, that they were all under arrest, that we had the advantage, but we would not harm them if they behaved themselves. Seeing that it was useless to resist, they settled down.

The captain then ordered them to kill a calf for us as we had not had anything to eat since noon the day before. They obeyed orders and we soon had a good breakfast. Later in the day part of our men went out and searched through their herds. A good many cattle and horses belonging to our men were found among them.

The leaders of the outlaws were not in this band. They were off making another raid somewhere. One of the band of outlaws was deaf and dumb. Captain Rich took this fellow aside and carried on a conversation with him by writing. From the man he learned that the rest of the band were expected in that night, but as they didn't come, we concluded that they had seen us and were lying off in the hills waiting a chance to ambush us and rescue their comrades. We were too sharp to give them the chance to do that. For three days we waited, guarding our prisoners. Then, as we thought it too risky to try to take so large a band of desperate men through the rough timbered country, we must pass to get home, we took forty head of their horses as bond for their appearance at court in thirty days, and let the prisoners go.

When we were ready to set out, we carried their guns to the top of a hill, and Hoopes and I were left to guard the weapons till we were sure our men were far enough away to be safe; then we left the weapons and struck out for home after them.

As no one ever came to redeem the horses, they were sold at auction. This nest of outlaws was broken up for good the following year. Since then that part of the country has had no serious trouble with horse thieves and robbers.

One more rather exciting experience that befell me and then I shall close these stories of my life in the rugged West.

It happened during 1870. Jim Donaldson, Charley Webster, or "Webb," as we called him, and I were taking a peddling trip to Fort Stanbow, the soldier post that was temporarily established near South Pass for the protection of the miners and emigrants. We had loaded up our three wagons with butter, eggs and chickens.

The Sioux Indians were then on the warpath. We had been warned to keep an eye on our horses, but we thought little about it till one day we were nooning on the Big Sandy—about where Lot Smith burnt the government wagon trains—when, just as we sat down to eat, "Webb" looked up to see our horses, which we had turned loose to graze, disappearing in a cloud of dust. Two Indians were behind them, both on an old horse of mine, and they were whooping the others across the hills to beat time.

Jumping to our feet we dashed after them afoot. This was useless of course. "Webb" and Donaldson jerked out their revolvers and took several shots at the rascals, but they were out of revolver reach and getting farther away every second, while we stared and damned them.

It was a pretty pickle we were in — forty miles from nowhere, with three wagons loaded with perishable stuff, and not a horse to move them. We got madder and madder as we watched the thieving devils gradually slip out of sight beyond the sand hills.

Then we went back to our wagons—cussing and discussing the situation. For an hour or more we tried to puzzle a way out of our difficulty. It was no use. The more we worried the worse it looked. All the money I had was invested in those eggs and butter and they would soon be worse than nothing in the hot sun. The other boys were in as bad a fix as I was. We just couldn't see a way out of it; but we kept up our puzzling till suddenly we heard a rumbling noise.

A few minutes later a covered wagon drawn by a pair of mules came in sight.

An old man—"Boss Tweed" the boys had nicknamed him—was the driver. In the seat with him was a boy, who had a saddle horse tied behind. They were surely a welcome sight to us.

We told them of our trouble. The old man reckoned he could help us out. He proposed that we load the supplies of two of our wagons on his larger wagon, then trailing our other wagon behind, his old mules he thought could haul us into South Pass. It looked like our only chance, but "Webb" thought he had a better plan.

The Indians, he said must make their way out of the country through a certain pass. There was no other route they could escape by. If we three would take the mules and the boy's horse and ride hard through the night we might get ahead of the thieves and retake our horses.

"Anything for the best," said the old man; but the boy objected. We shouldn't take his horse. He started to untie his animal, but we stopped him. Our situation was a desperate one; he had to give in.

We unhitched the mules, and strapped quilts on their backs. Donaldson and I jumped on them; "Webb took the horse. Then we struck the trail single file, my old mule on lead with Jim to whip him up and "Webb" behind him to whip Jim's mule. It was a funny sight. I never meet Jim but he calls up that circus parade loping along over the hills out on the Big Sandy.

The old mules were slow, but they were tough. They kept up their steady gait mile after mile through the night. We couldn't see any trail—just the gap in the mountains against the sky to guide us as we loped and jogged and jogged and loped through the long night.

When daylight came to light our way, we found ourselves at the place where the trail took up over the pass. Soon it forked, the two branches of the trail going up two ravines which were separated by a low, narrow ridge. We saw no fresh tracks on either trail so we knew the Indians had not passed this point. It looked as if we had got ahead of them as ''Webb'' hoped.

We rode up one ravine about a mile from the forks, keeping out of the trail so as to leave no tracks to alarm the thieves if they came our way. Here we stopped and ''Webb'' went up on the ridge to where he could overlook the country and at the same time watch both trails. Our plan was to wait till we found out which trail the Redskins took then we could post ourselves on either trail and head them off as they came up the one or the other ravine, it being but a short distance between the trails.

''Webb'' had not been on watch long before he sighted them coming about six miles away. He waited till they reached the forks. Luck favored us. They took our trail. Seeing this ''Webb'' slipped down to tell us. We hastily hid our horses in the tall brush that bordered the little creek, chose a place where the big birches hung over the trail and got ready. "Webb" and Donaldson, having revolvers, were to take the lead Indian, while with my rifle I was to settle accounts with the other.

We hadn't long to wait till here they came crowding our horses full tilt along the trail. We held ourselves till we had the dead drop on them then we all fired. My companions both caught their Indian in the head. I took mine right under the arm. Their horses jumped and they both tumbled off so dead they didn't know what struck them. It might seem a hard thing to do, but we were not going to take any chances.

I never have found any joy in killing Indians. And I never have killed any except when circumstances compelled it; Nor have I ever felt like boasting about such bloody work. These rascals certainly deserved what they got. They had stolen all we had and left us in a very serious difficulty. They were Sioux Indians who were escaping from a battle with the soldiers of Fort Stanbow.

You can easily believe we were mighty glad to get back those horses and strike the trail again towards our wagons. We found things all right there. The old man had taken good care of our produce while we were away. He was just as happy as we were over our success. But do you think he would take any pay for his trouble. Not a cent. "It was pay enough," he said, "to feel so good because he had helped us out of a bad fix." When we got to South Pass, however, we found his home and left him some supplies with our good wishes. He was away at the time so he couldn't object.

The boy who had refused us his horse didn't object though to taking five dollars for his pay. I've always found a heap of difference among the human beings one meets in his travels.

The years that have followed these wild days have not been so filled with exciting edventures, yet no year has passed without its rough and trying experiences; for it has been my lot to live always on the frontier. Even now my home is in Jackson's Hole—one of the last of our mountain valleys to be settled. In 1889 I first went into this beautiful valley, and a few years later, I pioneered the little town now called Wilson, in my honor.

It was here that I was brought again into close contact with my Shoshone friends—the Indians from whom for many years, I had been all but lost. In 1895, when the so-called Jackson's Hole Indian war broke out and several Indians were killed and others captured and brought to trial for killing game, I was called on to act as interpreter. My sympathies went out to the Indians at this time. They were misunderstood and mistreated as they always have been. The Indian has always been pushed aside, driven and robbed of his rights.

It is a sad thought with me to see the Red men giving away so rapidly before our advancing civilization. Where thousands of the Indians once roamed free, only a scattered few remain. The old friends of my boyhood days with Washakie have almost entirely passed away. Only once in a great while do I find one who remembers Yagaiki, the little boy, who once lived with their old chief's mother. But when I do happen to meet one—as I did last year when I found Hans, a wealthy Indian, who lives now on his ranch at the Big Bend in Port Neuf Canyon—then we have a good time, I tell you, recalling the days of long ago when Uncle Nick was among the Shoshones.